Policy Implementation

Subject Leadership

Principles and Practice

Policy Implementation

Elizabeth Hoult

This book is dedicated to Penny.

© Optimus Publishing 2004

Elizabeth Hoult asserts the moral right to be identified as the author of this work.

The information contained in this publication is believed to be correct at the time of going to press. Whilst care has been taken to ensure that the information is accurate, the publisher can accept no responsibility for any errors or omissions or for changes to the details given.

A CIP catalogue record for this book is available from the British Library.

Designed by:
Character Design
Highridge
Lower Wrigglebrook Lane
Kingsthorne
Hereford HR2 8AW
Tel: 01981 541154

Printed by:
Black Bear Press Limited
King's Hedges Road
Cambridge CB4 2PQ
Tel: 01223 424571

Published by Optimus Publishing,
A trading name of Electric Word plc
67-71 Goswell Road
London EC1V 7EP
Registration number 3934419

ISBN: 0-9542519-9-7

Acknowledgements

I am grateful to the subject leaders with whom I have worked on the Diploma in Subject Leadership since 1998; their thoughts and accounts of experiences have inspired and informed me. Thanks as well to the team at Optimus, to Kit Field for his insights, encouragement and knowledge, and to the authors of the other books in this series for their ideas.

Thanks to Simon for his insights and for his patience in hearing about work in progress.

Contents

List of tasks

Glossary

Cats	Cognitive Assessment Tests
CEDP	Career Entry and Development Profile
CPD	Continuing Professional Development
EAL	English as an Additional Language
GTC	General Teacher Council
HOD	Head of Department
ICT	Information and Communication Technology
Inset	In-service Training
ITE	Initial Teacher Education
LEA	Local Education Authority
LMS	Local Management of Schools
LSA	Learning Support Assistant
NCSL	National College for School Leadership
NPQH	National Professional Qualification for Headship
NQT	Newly Qualified Teacher status
Ofsted	Office for Standards in Education
QCA	Qualifications and Curriculum Authority
QTS	Qualified Teacher Status
Sats	Standard Assessment Tasks
Senco	Special Educational Needs Coordinator
SMT	Senior Management Team
TTA	Teacher Training Agency

Introduction to the subject leadership series

Subject leaders and middle managers are required increasingly to work at a strategic as well as an operational level. This involves a clear understanding of their role, and also technical skills to perform their function. The impact of effective subject leadership is becoming more and more known. Ofsted reports have identified subject leadership as a key role in schools, and the development of middle manager programmes in higher education institutions and local authorities has proliferated in recent years. The National College for School Leadership (NCSL) has begun to 'roll out' the 'Leading from the Middle' programme, providing a blended learning approach for middle and emerging leaders.

This new series is designed to reflect the full range of demands made upon middle managers and to provide practical guidance on how subject leaders should operate. The series complements *Subject Leadership – A Key Reference File* (Field *et al,* 2001). This reference file contains guidance and information of what subject leaders should do as leaders of curriculum areas and also as middle managers in schools. This new series does not simply target those following courses and programmes, but also aims to challenge and inform those in role, and those aspiring to the positions of subject leaders. As individual texts, authors have striven to provide guidance and to lead the reader to a level of understanding that helps subject leaders to recognise the potential and impact of their work.

The aim is to make explicit principles of good practice for subject leaders, working on the premise that as professionals, subject leaders and indeed other middle managers should be empowered to adapt and tailor good practice to fit within their own working circumstances.

Subject leadership is developing as a role. Glynn Kirkham's text, *The Role of the Subject Leader,* is designed to assist subject leaders in the establishment of a detailed appreciation of the role. The text also serves to identify the qualities, attributes and knowledge necessary to fulfil the role with confidence. Glynn provides a comprehensive guide to the demands made upon subject leaders and middle managers, demonstrating the breadth of expertise required to work effectively. Glynn is also keen to assist subject leaders to be empowered to lead, rather than just to respond to initiatives.

In this book Elizabeth Hoult addresses the place of subject leaders in devising and implementing policy. The very terms 'middle manager' and 'subject leader' reflect the tensions within the role. Elizabeth examines the extent to which those in post are able to 'lead' – direct practice through policy development, and the extent to which they 'manage' – implementing policy from government, LEAs and the whole school. The subject leader has to be both responsive and proactive. Elizabeth's text provides support in coping and mastering such a dichotomy.

Simon Hughes' text, *Resource Management*, deals with all aspects of managing resources, and he argues against a piecemeal approach to what may be perceived as day-to-day administrative tasks. Simon acknowledges the complexity of resource management, and provides a range of strategic vantage points, which support the leadership role of subject leaders in this area.

In *The Cross-Curriculum*, Kit Field considers the contribution subject leaders make to the whole school and the whole curriculum. Kit acknowledges that each subject leader has a unique contribution to make, and a collaborative role, in providing for a single, broad and relevant curriculum. Subject teaching cannot, and should not operate in isolation, and Kit argues that there should be attention given to the underlying values and purposes. This, Kit believes, provides subject leaders with a reason for middle management, which extends beyond assuring the best examination results.

The four authors are experts in the field of middle management. A common theme which fuelled the selection of content, and which is shared by the authors, is that subject leaders are crucial and key people in schools. To a large extent their effectiveness determines the success of a school. The belief is that in combination, subject leaders drive the curriculum of a school, and therefore the impact of their work is immense. All the authors see subject leaders as professionals who should work as a team, in collaboration with a school's senior management teams. Middle managers they believe should be proactive and display leadership qualities. Within a sound and efficient management structure, middle managers play one of the most important roles in a school. The writers are aware that much in education originates from the centre, and that it could be perceived that teachers have decreasing control of subject content, pedagogy and assessment strategies. However, the tide could be turning, and the authors in this series aim to play a part in the re-professionalisation of teachers, and in particular of subject leaders and middle managers.

Kit Field,
Series Editor

Preface

Subject Leadership Principles and Practice: Policy Implementation is one of a series of books. The series has been developed as an outcome of the text *Subject Leadership: A Key Reference File*. The file provided the reader with a detailed account of what subject leaders should do, drawing on government documentation and the national *Standards for Subject Leaders* in particular. The books in this series each take a theme contained within the file to develop *principles of good practice*.

The changes in education of the 1980s and the 1990s were so rapid, and in many cases so radical, that it has taken some time to grasp the full implications for teachers at particular stages of their careers. Some teachers have found themselves in professional roles that have little or no resemblance to those adopted by their counterparts 20 years earlier. A good deal of research (eg Docking, 1999; Ball, 1994) has examined the wider impact of these changes – on society, schools and the profession. This book will concentrate on what policy changes have meant for one group of teachers: the subject leaders.

There has been a growth of interest in middle management in schools. This is partly a result of the changes to the management of schools brought about by the introduction of Local Management of Schools (LMS) and a new inspection system by the Conservative government, and of the enduring emphasis on accountability and the commitment to the notion of leadership by the New Labour government. There has also been a consequent increase in texts directed at subject leaders in schools (Field *et al*, 2000; Bell and Ritchie, 1999; Blandford, 1997 etc). Some of these texts are linked directly to the *Standards for Subject Leaders* (TTA, 1998, at www.canteach.gov.uk), as is this one. This book aims to offer practical advice for subject leaders on how to juggle competing responsibilities and to empower themselves in the light of policy changes that have an impact on their work. It also seeks to help subject leaders to develop and implement policies which directly or indirectly enhance the quality of learning in their subject area.

Since 1998, teachers in England have been working with a new professional development framework. That year saw the introduction of a standards-based framework of professional development for teachers, which was a major shift from the largely competence-based model that preceded it. As a result teachers in England are now required to demonstrate their attainment of standards by presentation of evidence. For many teachers this will involve compiling a portfolio. This contrasts with the previous system in which teachers were simply required to demonstrate that the processes of professional development were being undertaken, rather than demonstrating the outcomes. The new framework includes a whole tranche of standards including those for Qualified Teacher Status (QTS), Newly Qualified Teachers (NQTs), Sencos, the standards for headteachers, SEN specialist standards and standards associated with threshold and advanced skills (Field, 2002a). They are designed to mark the progress of teachers in different stages of their professional development from qualifying to headship.

These *Standards* form the background of this book – not only because they are the statutory guidelines for the professional development of subject leaders but also because they have a good many useful things to say about subject leadership. They should not, however, be regarded as definitive. We will glean the important points from the *Standards* regarding policy but we will also examine them critically in the light of the research literature and experience.

Who will benefit from this book?

This book is written for you if you are interested in subject leadership. You might already be in a subject leadership position or you may be aspiring to that role. The term 'subject leadership' is used because that is the term used in the *Standards for Subject Leaders*. It is a somewhat problematic term, though, and we will examine the reasons for this later on in the book. This book will be of interest to teachers in other middle management roles as well. You may have been carrying out this role for a number of years or you may have been recently appointed. Whatever your situation, this book is designed to guide you through the policy-writing process.

Interesting work has been carried out into the role of the middle manager in schools (Field *et al*, 2000; West, 1998; and Harris, 1999 among others) and although this book is underpinned by theoretical arguments and research findings, it is not designed to be an academic tract. Rather, it is a book aimed directly at practitioners with real dilemmas regarding policy. To this end I would like to make two points about the text.

Firstly, I address the reader directly throughout the book because reference can be made to practice more directly that way. Secondly, each chapter includes tasks. These are inextricably bound to the subject matter contained in that chapter and they are designed to help the reader to learn from the chapter. There are individual and team tasks. The individual tasks are designed to be completed by you, the reader, individually. They help you to reflect on your own practice and to construct a way forward. The team tasks, by contrast, are to be used with your team (or with any group with whom you are engaged in policy-writing). Their purpose is to help you guide development activities and meetings and they will help you to develop the learning of the whole team regarding policy-writing.

Each chapter is divided into three sections: **regulatory**, in which the policy framework within which subject leaders must operate is set out (these sections particularly refer to the *Standards for Subject Leaders*); **discussion**, in which various research perspectives are considered; and **operational**, in which a guide for how subject leaders can implement these ideas in the real world is put forward. The book aims to help subject leaders use theory to explore and to find a clear way to solving practical dilemmas.

The first three chapters situate the subject leader's role within the wider political context. In chapter 1, I explore some of the idiosyncrasies of subject leadership pursuits and how they differ from the tasks carried out by other professionals in a school. In chapters 2 and 3, I examine government policy since 1988 and its effect on teachers in general, and subject leaders in particular, in terms of shifting boundaries and workload. Thereafter the focus of the book is how subject leaders can excel within this context. Although there are plenty of useful, practical suggestions in the operational sections of each chapter, the tone of the book is not imperative: there are far too many people already telling teachers what to do.

Rather, these suggestions offer practical ways forward in a sometimes confused and confusing political landscape.

In the last two chapters I develop a view of the role of the subject leader as not just subject to change but also as an agent of it. Finally I turn the focus back towards the subject leader as an individual and I place professional development at the heart of this change process.

A word on phases: subject leadership is a cross-phase concept and the book is intended to be helpful to teachers in primary, middle and secondary schools. There are significant differences between the role of the subject leader in various schools, though, and these differences will be explored in the various chapters. Some points will be most useful to subject leaders in secondary schools and large primary schools where the role is remunerated and the subject leader is given proper managerial responsibility for policy implementation.

Finally, the book is linked to the *Standards for Subject Leaders* and these standards are intended for use in England and Wales. Although the book will be of interest to teachers from other countries the standards referred to are directed at teachers in England and Wales.

What is special about subject leadership?

Chapter 1

> **Objectives**
>
> This chapter sets out the issues and challenges facing subject leaders in a general way. Each matter is explored at more length later on in the book. By the end of this chapter you will have:
>
> - explored the meaning of policy
>
> - considered the two types of policy that have an impact on subject leaders – internal and external policy – and briefly examined the inherent tensions for subject leaders
>
> - considered the dilemmas facing subject leaders concerning the implementation of policy.

1.1 Regulatory

The Standards for Subject Leaders (TTA, 1998) forms the main statutory framework for subject leaders' professional development and role definition. Although much of the information contained within it may be found elsewhere, it defines the extent of the role of a subject leader in a way that is unprecedented. The TTA (1998, p1) states that the purpose of the *Standards* is that it 'set out the professional knowledge, understanding, skills and attributes necessary to carry out effectively key tasks of that role. It is the sum of these aspects which defines the expertise demanded of the role in order to achieve the outcomes set out in the standards.'

The *Standards* are, essentially, a professional development framework, intended as a set of signposts for teachers thinking about their own development and for professional development providers to plan activities accordingly. The *Standards* are not, therefore, . intended to be punitive. As much of what is described may be found as descriptions of good practice elsewhere, we can also assume that the ideas contained in the *Standards* will be used to inspect middle management in schools by Ofsted.

These are the important points contained in *The Standards for Subject Leaders* TTA, 1998:

1) Subject leaders should develop and monitor their own policies which contribute to the development of whole-school policies, including those on 'behaviour, discipline, bullying and racial harassment' (5Avi).

2) They will also have an ongoing monitoring role regarding the progress of their own subject policies (5Avii).

3) It is important that a clear subject policy exists for assessment (5Bv).

4) The headteacher, senior managers and governors need to be well informed about all subject policies (5Cx).

5) Subject leaders also have a managerial role and one of these duties is to 'performance manage' staff and to use the process to develop personal and professional effectiveness of the appraisees (5Civ).

6) Subject leaders will access and implement national policy as well as creating their own policies for their own subject areas. The *Standards* state that subject leaders should 'play a major role in the development of school policy and practice' (TTA, 1998, p4).

7) The ability to 'prioritise, plan and organise' (4a p4) is placed second on the list of skills and attributes required of subject leaders. This means participating in the development of policy at whole-school level, but also leading the process at departmental/subject level.

8) In addition to the statutory curriculum requirements for their subject, subject leaders should have knowledge and understanding of the following 'macro' policies and how they relate to internal school policy: literacy, numeracy and ICT skills (since conceptualised in the national strategy for key stage 3), as well as:
   - employment law, equal opportunities legislation, personnel, external relations, finance and change (i)
   - school governance and how it can contribute to the work of the subject leader (l)
   - implications of the Code of Practice for Special Needs for teaching and learning in their subject (n)
   - health and safety legislation (o)
   - assessment (c)
   - target-setting (f)
   - equal opportunities (i)

   Clearly the subject leader also needs to have a good understanding of how each of these national policy statements is applied at school level.

9) The *Standards* also inform us that subject leaders should be able to communicate effectively, orally and in writing, with the headteacher, other staff, pupils, parents, governors, external agencies and the wider community, including business and industry (4ci).

10) In addition to the *Standards*, the government has also stated in its policy for continuing professional development that teachers should keep abreast of national policy changes and developments. The General Teaching Council has stated in *The Teachers' Professional Learning Framework* (2003, p9) that 'working in a team' (for example, a subject team or department) supports professional learning.

1.2 Discussion

The term 'subject leader' includes teachers in traditional head-of-department posts in secondary schools as well as teachers who take the lead in a subject area in a primary school. In the case of the latter this teacher is often unremunerated and also has other subject responsibility areas. There has been, for some time, a proliferation of professional development courses aimed at 'middle management' – which is a general and all-embracing term. More recently discussions have included the use of the term 'subject leaders', which is a highly complex concept but used hereafter for simplicity because it is the language of the *Standards* document.

The term 'subject leadership' is very limiting. Firstly, it ignores the considerable group of middle managers in schools whose responsibility is pastoral or not subject-focused (such as those responsible for assessment or coordination in primary schools and heads of year in secondary schools). Secondly, the assumption seems to be that the word 'leadership' adequately describes the activities of a middle manager. It is well documented that many of the activities of middle managers are administrative and managerial tasks and that 'leadership' represents only a small proportion of the overall workload. Thirdly, the cross-phase application of the term assumes erroneously that the role is the same in primary, middle and secondary schools. This is not the case.

The manager in the middle

As a subject leader you are in an interesting but inherently variegated position in the management structure of a school. Along with senior management you need to be able to access and implement national (or 'macro') policy as well as creating your own internal policies. The demands are different from those experienced by most senior managers, though. The personal challenges of being a teacher with an often unrelieved timetable, as well as taking on a leadership role, are considerable. The issues surrounding workload are significant and it means that there is a great need for efficient time management. To a certain extent, the *Standards for Subject Leaders* acknowledge the challenging situation that characterises the working conditions of a subject leader. They state that the effectiveness of a headteacher will have an impact on that of the subject leader (5A) and that 'the way in which decisions, policies and practices are communicated and implemented throughout the school' (TTA, 1998) will also affect the subject leader's effectiveness. In other words, it is not just that internal as well as external policies will affect subject leaders but that the quality of those policies will also have a big impact on your work too.

This presents us with one of the big questions facing subject leaders in school: is it possible to develop a distinctive and personal leadership style even if it conflicts with the dominant style of the senior managers of the school? The *Standards* can give the impression that this is possible but subject leaders reading this will know that it is a highly problematic business. For example, you may work for a very authoritarian headteacher and this means that you are operating in a specific leadership culture. If the autocratic headteacher avoids delegation and tends to create policies apparently on the hoof, without much consultation, then obviously this will have a knock-on effect on the way you create and implement policies with the subject team. If this describes your situation then you will need to find a way of creating a more collaborative culture within the team without offending the headteacher. Herein lies the central problem facing the subject leader. You can do a lot to effect change and high standards within your own subject area but you are always working in the context of a wider leadership culture.

What's in a name?

It could be argued that the term 'middle management' is inappropriate because not only does it present a multi-layered role as if it were a one-dimensional unit but also it is a misnomer. The term 'middle manager' defines the role in terms of its administrative and leadership responsibilities. In fact, nearly all middle managers are still engaged in teaching for the largest proportion of their working days. In this sense the professional whose main role is teaching is defined by the more peripheral aspects of his or her job.

So how do you define yourself? Are you a middle manager, a subject coordinator or a subject leader? Are you a senior manager in training? The debate may sound somewhat esoteric in the busy schoolday when getting things done will seem more important than how you define your role but it has significant implications not only for how you carry out your role, and what that role includes, but also for your subject.

The National College for School Leadership, the centre dedicated to enhancing the development of leadership skills in the education population, has recently set up its own programme for middle managers – *Leading from the Middle*. One of its 10 leadership propositions is that 'Leadership should be dispersed throughout the school community'. It refers to the middle cohort as 'emergent leaders' and the term includes a wider group than just subject leaders; key stage coordinators, pastoral leaders, Sencos and those with a cross-curricular responsibility are also included.

This indicates a shift in understanding. Firstly, instead of leadership being associated entirely with senior management there is a recognition that leadership skills in the middle are fundamental to school improvement. Secondly, it is recognised that the middle rung of emergent leaders will also include a range of professionals who do not fit into the traditional secondary school model of middle management but who nevertheless play a very important role in the school's leadership structure. Gunter (2001, pp106-107) correctly states that 'The complexity of teachers' work means that activity may not always be organised into a sub-unit such as a department, but may entail whole-school coordination such as pastoral work'. We only need reflect for a couple of minutes about the complexity of tasks carried out by a subject leader in a lunch period to illustrate this point.

Challenges facing the subject leader

Gunter (2001, p137) argues that when teachers, including those with formal leadership roles, are unhappy about their working lives we must not dismiss this as 'eccentric conservatism' which can easily be cured by a 'how to' guide to management. So it is important to explore the problems thoroughly before thinking about solutions. Some of the challenges facing you, therefore, include:

1) conflicting commitments (how do you weigh your various priorities as subject leader, pastoral tutor or classroom teacher etc?)

2) the tension between accountability but no apparent responsibility for staff teaching the subject (this is true of many primary colleagues and secondary colleagues who have senior members of staff teaching part-time in the department)

3) the conflicting roles of management and teaching and the resultant 'squeezing' of time.

The following chapters do not attempt to solve the problems that you face in schools. Nor do they pretend that combining subject leadership with an already demanding professional role is easy. Running through the book, however, is an attempt to articulate and conceptualise the issues for teachers in the middle and to point to some ways of using theoretical perspectives to develop your work and role.

Task 1	Time and the subject leader

INDIVIDUAL TASK

Use the table below to chart how you spend your time. Take any typical lunch period this week and make a note of all the separate interactions that you have during that time. Include all conversations of a professional nature, even if you are eating your lunch while you are having them. For each interaction attach an approximate time. Now divide the interactions into categories as they relate to your professional role – class teacher, subject leader, pastoral leader etc. Reflect on the results – what do they tell you about how your role is defined? How can the proportions be modified? This task is designed to help you understand the nature of your role and to help you to use it to achieve your goals.

The complexity of the subject leader's role

Task	Time spent	Classification (classroom teaching/subject leadership, admin/leadership etc)

1.3   The characteristics of effective leadership

It could be argued that in the past some teachers who were promoted to head-of-department levels were promoted on the strength of their teaching ability rather than their potential to manage well. Some heads of departments, consequently, regarded themselves as administrators rather than managers with significant responsibility for the motivation and monitoring of staff. This is changing.

Research by Harris (2001) into effective departments has concluded that across the curriculum effective departments are characterised by 'aims and policies clearly set out in a departmental handbook and supported by well-ordered planning and administration'. The policies are not overly bureaucratic, though. Rather, these effective departments are led by good subject leaders who 'promulgate their vision of what they want to achieve in a variety of ways. For example, they set out their aims and strategies in a considered and realistic policy document that articulates the department's purposes and systems, subsuming national curriculum and other requirements within a framework that remains distinctive.' What is being advocated here is a view of policy that is both a tool for and illustrative of effective team management.

The good departments do not use policies as a substitute for good practice – they are tangible evidence of good practice. 'Paperwork' can be seen as the proof of efficiency. But this is not necessarily the case. In fact the opposite can be true. Glover *et al* (1998) argue that 'Many subject leaders confuse administration with leadership and take refuge in their administrative work to avoid some of the inevitable problems arising, for example, from enhanced monitoring and evaluation of the work of professional colleagues'. This is time and over-writing can be counter-productive. We should take our cue from Keats when he says 'I have come to this resolution – never to write for the sake of writing'.

1.4   Policy and politics

Our working definition of policy is 'the means by which principles and values are made explicit in practical terms'. In practice, though, this may be too simple. In general the word 'policy' can mean both a governing principle and an insurance document. In the early days of Ofsted, many headteachers perceived pressure from inspection teams to create paperwork and to close all possible gaps. Many responded by providing a great deal of evidence of good practice. Policies were ostensibly created as manifestations of governing principles but in fact were being used as insurance policies or safety nets to protect against being judged by Ofsted as not complying with national regulations. This is because the need for a policy can be interpreted by schools as the need to have something written on paper for the sake of external scrutiny.

Many policies are not the written manifestations of principles and practices that they should be. At their worst they can be a diluted statement of what school managers think that the policy should be. Practice, however, remains a complex set of interactions and that is part of the problem with policies. Fullan (1991, p118) tells us that the working life of the teacher is incredibly complex: 'Starting where teachers are means starting with routine, overload, and limits to reform because this is the situation for most teachers'. It is simplistic, then, to think that we can even describe this practice in a written policy, let alone convey deep-rooted philosophical standpoints at the same time.

Different discourses always compete in a piece of writing, oratory or even conversation so that the most powerful voice is heard. Inevitably this means that other voices will be suppressed. The rather anodyne, bureaucratic view of policies as necessary paperwork within school structures can disguise this aspect of power struggle in the policy-writing process. Many policies espouse a viewpoint on professional practice that is covertly *political*. In other words, policies always emanate from an ideological standpoint, whether their authors acknowledge this is the case or not. An example of this would be the competing ideologies that led to the national curriculum.

Task 2	Your learning autobiography

INDIVIDUAL TASK

Write a learning autobiography in which you set down your own history of learning in the subject that you lead. Think about when you first were taught it and try to remember your own experience of the subject at school. How do you feel about it now? Do you have any contact with the subject outside school (does it coincide with any hobbies etc)? Are you a member of professional associations linked to your subject?

There is often a marked difference in the responses to this task from primary and secondary colleagues. Secondary teachers have usually chosen to pursue their study of the subject and have a degree in it. Primary colleagues, on the other hand, often simply 'end up' with responsibility for a subject that they have no particular interest in. This task is especially pertinent for you if you are in the latter situation because it will help to recognise and articulate your feelings about the subject before we proceed.

Professor Brian Cox led the panel that created the first national curriculum for English. He set out to discover from teachers of English, at all stages of compulsory schooling, what the ideological and philosophical principles were in their teaching. Instead of finding one dominant ideological position, though, he discovered that at least five ideological stances were at work in English teaching. These tended to co-exist within English departments in secondary schools and in discussions among primary schoolteachers. 'Cox's five models of the English teacher' informed the national curriculum of 1992 and was an attempt to bring all five models together. It was not an attempt to find a compromise between the five models – rather to let them all co-exist. Cox argued that there was not a problem with ideological difference as long as each stance was recognised and respected by the others.

The citizenship curriculum is another interesting example of how ideology and policy are linked. The curriculum was designed with a plethora of different lobby groups in mind. The resulting document (DfEE, 1999) is remarkably wide and open to interpretation because it aims not to exclude the lobby groups represented. Consequently schools may be fairly liberal in their interpretation of it. This is an example of how macro policy has consciously been influenced and shaped by ideology and yet it has been opened up rather than closed down as a result.

Policies, therefore, are influenced by a combination of values and ideologies that emanate from general culture, national government, community, school, department, the public. Thus they are often much less simple than they purport to be.

Eleanor Rawlings (2001) has examined the impact of macro policy decisions on geography over the years and she convincingly argues that ideology has had an impact on the formation of the geography curriculum. But she warns against overstressing the impact (p145). 'Macro level struggles may have resulted in less than perfect curriculum frameworks in school geography, but creative curriculum development at micro level is still a feasible strategy'. There is an important message here for subject leaders. It is possible to find ways to adapt the curriculum to the team's philosophy of the integrity of the subject. In other words, to compromise. There is a danger, though, that by continually taking this approach subject leaders may risk losing their professional power to reflect on and ultimately reject macro policy interventions.

In a major study into teachers' sense of their professional selves, Moore *et al* (2002) discovered that a response to the sweeping and extensive policy changes of the past two decades has been that many teachers have adopted a pragmatic approach to their professional role. The authors argue that this could be seen as a good thing – a desire by teachers to simply get on with the job. More worryingly, though, it could be argued that 'teachers are buying into a political discourse of pragmatism in which the inclination to mobilise for active, collective political opposition is diverted... to more isolated engagements in the internal politics in their own institutions'. This pessimism is picked up by Gold *et al* (2002). They argue that 'Emergent leaders rarely have the opportunity to make links outside the school except within their subject or area of responsibility' and that they are therefore unlikely to influence policy in a significant way from the middle.

In this sense there is no distinction between the subject leader's response to internal and external policy. All policy change is engaged with, subverted or rejected on the level of intervention from the hierarchy. It brings into question the idea of autonomy because if the level of self-determination afforded to the headteacher is already compromised then the freedom for the subject leader to interpret these policies and create his or her own subject-specific policies in the light of them must be negligible.

Indeed, the idea that there is a dichotomy facing the subject leader between internal and external policy may also be naïve. Helen Gunter (2001) disputes whether the headteacher is creating internal policy: 'the mandated models of school leadership, as we have seen, are not about educational leadership but about enabling the headteacher to be a middle manager to both implement and be accountable for centrally directed policy'.

It is true that an ongoing paradox runs through the *Standards for Subject Leaders*. Several times in the text subject leaders are encouraged to develop their own leadership styles but at the same time much is also made of interpreting national policy and making use of national assessment data and inspection findings. We need to be critical of the notion that subject leaders have valid jurisdiction to create their own policies in the first place. There will be more about the complexities of the role of the subject leader within a management hierarchy later.

1.5 Internal and external policy

We have established that both macro (national/LEA) and micro (school-specific) policy have an effect on the work of subject leaders. The *Standards for Subject Leaders* state that there are certain elements of knowledge and understanding that should form a part of the subject leader's professional repertoire. This is interesting because the case seems to be advanced for a body of 'professional knowledge' which should be practical as well as technical. Subject leaders should have knowledge and understanding of, among other things, a school's 'action plans'. This is an interesting departure from the usual terminology, 'development plan' (MacGilchrist *et al*, 1995). The term action plan, however, seems to be more resonant of the post-Ofsted action plan and so closer to the DfES machine.

Subject leaders should also be able to understand and have knowledge of 'national and international standards of achievement in the subject' to 'inform expectations'. This does not necessarily equip teachers to understand local features. There is a question to be raised here about the extent to which international findings could and should be used by those of us who have limited knowledge of the principles of comparative education.

Key ideas about school effectiveness and school improvement (Hargreaves *et al,* 1993) are maintained throughout this section. The philosophical background for the document, as it emerges, oscillates at times between **school effectiveness** (with the emphasis on improving the academic chances of pupils whose social and economic circumstances would suggest underachievement) and **school improvement** (where the capacity of a school to develop and change is highly prized). The inherent tensions between the characteristics required to 'add value' to classroom processes (the measurement of which is often based on summative assessments) and the need to build the capacity for continual development and improvement of professional practice mean that subject leaders might be forgiven for feeling that the *Standards* do not take sufficient account of the reality of the working day. A key area of professional knowledge, for example, is how to use 'comparative data', to 'understand benchmarks' and to set 'targets' (Hargreaves *et al,* 1993, p6). At the same time a 'key outcome' of good subject leadership is a senior management team who 'understand the needs of the subject' (Hargreaves *et al,* 1993, p5). The responsibility may well fall to the subject leader to articulate the needs of the subject to those higher up the chain of command, but any observer of real schools will be able to confirm that some highly effective subject leaders are still unable to ensure that their headteachers understand or act with reference to the needs of the subject or use this information to make 'greater improvements in the whole school's development'. Indeed, if the head of the school habitually adopts an adversarial or authoritarian style of leadership (Collarbone and Billingham, 1998) it may be impossible for the subject leader to make his or her voice heard, regardless of how effective he or she may be.

Another interesting paradox in the *Standards* is the ambivalence of the attitude towards the LEA. Some of the initiatives and drives for change are clearly depicted as being initiated at central government level. However, the document is notable and may be regarded as significantly different from any documents from the previous administration because it consistently includes the LEA as a reference point. Subject leaders should have knowledge and understanding of 'the implications of information and guidance documents from LEAs... and other national bodies and associations'. It is interesting and noteworthy that the LEA is placed first in the list here. Recent commentators (for example Bush, 2003) have suggested that the government may deploy yet more funds directly to schools, thus attenuating the role of the LEA even further.

The basic assumption that the subject leader will be working within the context of an effective school is continued in this section. Subject leaders should develop policies 'which reflect the school's commitment to high achievement'. It raises some interesting questions about an individual's professional development in the context of a low-achieving school which, in the language of school improvement, could be described as 'stuck' or by the government's term 'failing'. Fullan (1991, p315) argues that '...the evidence is that beginning teachers will get better or worse depending on the schools in which they teach', and one limitation of the *Standards* that is beginning to emerge is the lack of the acknowledgement of the part that school culture and contextual specificity play in the development and achievement of teachers.

The DfES (www.dfes.gov.uk), QCA (www.qca.org.uk) and Ofsted (www.ofsted.gov.uk) websites provide teachers with the opportunity to download policies directly. This means that subject leaders are able to gain access to national policy directives without going through the mediation of senior management. A disadvantage of this, however, is that a collective professional response to new policy and policy changes is sometimes not formulated before a strategic response is in place.

1.6 Operational

1) Do not punish yourself for not getting all the things done in a day that you feel that you ought to. Instead acknowledge the complexity of the task ahead of you.

2) Recognise the culture (and sub-cultures) and dominant forms of management style in school. This does not mean that you have to either reject or comply with these styles. It is useful, though, to know the context within which you operate.

3) Get a firm grip of your own philosophy of the subject. Think about what it means to you in terms of your own as well as the students' learning.

How does your own philosophy of the subject link to other members of the team? Ideally the policy should be created as a team effort. A good deal of talk will need to go on before the policy is put onto paper. This process itself can be a useful management tool in that it can help to bring the team together. The most effective types of whole-school development plans are those that are created in a collegial way – in other words, where effective teamwork has led to the creation of the policy. This will be dealt with in more detail in chapters 5 and 6. There is less research available about the process of policy creation at subject team or department level but we might safely extrapolate from whole-school findings that a well-led team approach may be the best one.

Now begin to think about your own values in relation to the subject and your leadership style. In a very practical sense policies also lend power to the subject leader because he or she may turn to the policy in a case of non-compliance on the part of another member of staff or to resolve a dispute. We have already seen the way that the *Standards for Subject Leaders* refer to employment law and the appraisal process. Many subject leaders in the past in both primary and secondary schools have not worked in this managerial way with members of their teams. The decisions left open to the subject leaders, therefore, are:

- what to teach and the sequencing of teaching and learning
- how the subject should be taught and learnt
- timetabling, to a certain extent
- the content of meetings.

We will examine the whole issue of management and leadership in chapter 5.

| Task 3 | Exploring ideological perspectives |

TEAM TASK

Present each person in the team with the following five statements and ask them to read them. Now ask the team to rank the statements according to whether or not they agree with them. Each team member should put the statement that he or she agrees with most strongly at the top and the one that they disagree with most strongly at the bottom of the list.

You may be surprised by the extent to which there is disagreement in the team. Do not worry about this – the purpose is to promote professional discussion rather than consensus at this stage.

Statements
- I believe that the way we teach our subject is inferior to the way it was taught when I was a pupil at school.
- I believe that our students get a great deal from our teaching. The methods we use are far superior to the way I was taught it.
- I believe that this subject's main purpose is to prepare students for adult life.
- I believe that we should be promoting the study of this subject for its own sake. Learning about our subject is a noble pursuit and does not need to be justified in other terms.
- Government interventions have improved the way that this subject is taught.

1.7 Summary

- The *Standards for Subject Leaders* stipulate that subject leaders should create and implement their own policies as well as having some input into whole-school policies. They will also access and interpret national policy in the context of their subject.
- Policy documents are pieces of writing and as such are products of a complex process.
- Subject leaders are subject to both internal and external policy although the distinction between the two may not be as great as first imagined.
- Policy documents are informed by ideology as well as the subjective experiences of those who create them.
- Policy documents will be effectively implemented and respected if they reflect a shared reality rather than the perceived reality of a minority interest group or one person.

Government policy

Chapter 2

Objectives

In the next chapter we will examine the specific national policy requirements that have an impact on the work of subject leaders. The subject of this chapter is the wider political context of educational policy developments.

By the end of this chapter you will have:

- understood the political context of the introduction of the national *Standards for Subject Leaders*

- considered a brief historical overview of national policy changes since 1988 as they relate to the work of subject leaders

- considered the current wider external policy framework within which subject leaders must operate

- understood the ways in which subject leaders can access and respond to national policy

- examined the various ways in which national policy can have an impact on the life and work of an individual school.

2.1 Regulatory

The main areas of policy since 1988 to affect subject leaders are:
- the national curriculum and the national assessment system
- open enrolment and the changing role of parents
- the introduction of the local management of schools and the move towards managerialism
- inspection and accountability
- increased emphasis on professional development and the redefinition of professionalism in the 1990s
- inclusion and the Race Relations (Amendment) Act, 2000.

All of these changes have meant that the role of the subject leader has changed radically from the head of department role of 15 or 20 years ago – as we discovered in the previous chapter. In fact the role of the subject leader in the primary school is a direct result of the introduction there of the national curriculum. Before its introduction, subject work was overseen by the class teacher (as it is now) but whole-school subject coordination was rare.

The *Standards*

In the introduction to the *Standards for Subject Leaders* we are told (p2) that 'The standards emphasise national priorities, particularly in support of the government's key educational targets in relation to literacy, numeracy and information and communications technology'. It is clear, then, that the *Standards* cannot be divorced from the political context within which they were created. The *Standards* have also been conceived as 'The basis for a more structured approach to appraisal, helping teachers and headteachers to set relevant targets, to assist in the evaluation of progress, to identify further development priorities and to confirm success'.

The subject leader should have knowledge and understanding of:
- management, including employment law, equal opportunities legislation, personnel, external relations, finance and change (3i, p6)
- the implications of the Code of Practice for Special Educational Needs for teaching and learning in their subject (3n, p6)
- the Race Relations (Amendment) Act, 2000.

The duty, which is obligatory, of schools under this latter act is that schools should take steps to eliminate unlawful racial discrimination, promote equal opportunities and promote good relations between people from different racial groups (section 71(1)). Schools have a duty to have in place a race equality policy. The policy should address the three areas outlined above. It will take the form of a written statement and, as with other policies, should be linked to an action plan for making the policy real and monitoring it.

Inspection framework

If you are a subject leader in a secondary school you should expect to be inspected by Ofsted as someone who is responsible for all the teaching of the subject in the school. This will usually involve a 'one-to-one' interview with a designated inspector as well as observation of teaching, inspection of schemes of work and of students' work. If you are a subject leader in a primary school, the inspection may well involve some of these but it will depend on the size of your school and the way that the head allocates responsibilities as to whether or not you are interviewed and so on.

2.2 Discussion

'English policy is to float lazily downstream, occasionally putting out a diplomatic hook to avoid collision.' So wrote Lord Salisbury in 1877. As far as education policy of the last two decades is concerned, nothing could be further from the truth than the image conjured above. Education policy has been more akin to crashing through the water. Diplomatic hooks have stayed firmly inside the boat. This is particularly true of the changes that have taken place since 1988.

1988 is significant because it was the year of the Education Reform Act. This piece of legislation brought with it the most far-reaching changes to schools since the 1944 Education Act. This move by the Conservative government centralised control of the content of the curriculum in a way that was unprecedented. It also made sweeping changes to the ways in which schools were managed. The local management of schools saw the reallocation of resources and capital from LEAs to schools. This was a gradual process and it laid the foundations for the local management of schools (LMS), open enrolment and grant-maintained schools. This aspect of the act was further developed in the Education Bill of 1993.

The aim of LMS was to give headteachers more autonomy. One of the results of this was that the concept of school leadership inevitably changed because along with

Task 4 | **Your professional biography**

INDIVIDUAL TASK

Trace your professional biography in the light of the changes in policy that have taken place since 1988. This will illustrate to you how profoundly government affects our professional lives. For each of the changes in policy listed below make a note of how it affected your life. It does not matter whether you have been a subject leader since 1988 or whether, in fact, you were still at school as a pupil in 1988.

Policy development	Impact on me
Introduction of national curriculum	
Removal of O-levels and CSEs and replacement with GCSEs	
Open enrolment	
Inspection framework	
LMS and grant-maintained schools	
Introduction of Sats	
Removal of student loans	
Inclusion	
National strategies including literacy strategy and the national strategy for key stage 3	
Introduction of new post-16 framework	
Introduction of framework for professional development	

autonomy goes accountability. Instead of the headteacher being regarded as the leading teaching professional in the school, heads were evolved into managers whose business was concerned as much with finance and contractual arrangements as it was with teaching and learning. As heads were distracted, subject leaders had to take on curriculum management in an unprecedented way. 1988 was a year of major political and cultural change that will still have a daily impact on your work as a subject leader.

2.3 The national curriculum and assessment

The national curriculum 'sets out a clear, full and statutory entitlement for all pupils. It determines the content of what will be taught, and sets attainment targets for learning. It also determines how performance will be assessed and reported' (DfEE, 1999, Foreword by the Secretary of State). Change is embedded in the very fabric of the national curriculum. It proclaims: 'the curriculum itself cannot remain static. It must be responsive to changes in society and in the economy, and in the nature of schooling itself' (p13).

The part of the 1988 Education Reform Act that was concerned with the content of the curriculum had a huge impact on teachers, especially those in the equivalent of subject leadership positions. As David Martin (Williams, 1995, p89) points out, 'the curriculum problem was further compounded because there was no overall view of the purposes of the curriculum except in terms of subjects'. For primary colleagues especially, this involved the enormous task of repositioning their professional practice in line with externally designed subject areas rather than a chronological understanding of child development in year groups.

The new national curriculum was a way of defining what could be taught and political power helped to shape it. The new way of working was not just about the content of lessons, though. The national curriculum also introduced attainment targets, against which pupils' performance was to be matched. The introduction of Sats and teacher-assessed levels made these levels of attainment 'official' and school performance could be monitored and compared in a way that had never happened before. Therefore subject leaders needed to have documentary evidence of what is going on in their subject area.

The emphasis on accountability has resulted in a significantly increased demand for policies from the subject leader and all policies will, to a certain extent, exist in order to protect the headteacher from external scrutiny.

Open enrolment

Another aspect of the 1988, 1992 and 1993 acts was the ideological drive to shift more power to parents to enable them to exert choice in the maintained sector. This introduced the concept of the market into the educational public sector. In the spirit of the marketplace that was defining a good deal of public policy in the late 1980s, the logical conclusion of open enrolment would have been the closure of the least popular schools as parents chose more 'successful' schools for their children and public funding was closely linked to subscription. Open enrolment also meant that schools were obliged to admit pupils up to capacity limit and that funding was attached to each pupil. As Kenneth Baker, then Secretary of State for Education, put it: 'I want to give people a chance to press for excellence; I want to give them the means to demand excellence; and I want to create a spur which will oblige the LEAs to deliver excellence' (Williams, 1995, p19).

This meant that parents could opt to withdraw their children from a school (and move them to another school) if they were unhappy with the level of provision. With the new funding arrangements, falling rolls would have an immediate and harsh impact on the school. It also elevated the position of the parent and gave parents a voice in the education of their offspring in an unprecedented way. This was consolidated following the Parents' Charter in 1991 and parents now have access to detailed information on the school's 'performance' and it placed teachers in new professional territory; they became vendors of learning. This legacy remains and subject leaders will still feel the impact of the reforms of the late 1980s and early 1990s, for example, subject leaders must sell the subject and the school.

This has meant that the old idea of a place in the neighbourhood school has virtually become obsolete. It could also be argued, though, that not a great deal has changed. For all the much-vaunted 'parents' right to choose', all that can actually happen is that parents can express a preference. There is no guarantee that the preference will lead to their choice being honoured.

The acts of 1998 and 1992 allowed schools to become more specialised (for example they could choose to become City Technology Colleges) and they gave parents more knowledge about schools than they had ever had before in the form of league tables.

The trajectory has continued in the New Labour administration with the diminishing role of the LEA and the introduction of specialist schools, beacon schools and foundation schools. The implication of all this for subject leaders is that their role is now inextricably linked to the need to 'sell' the subject to a range of stakeholders. Open evenings for prospective parents are no longer the relatively cosy events, serving a pastoral role, that they once were; they are full-scale marketing activities and the subject leader will feel the inevitable pressure to show his or her subject in the best possible light.

Inspection and accountability

Helen Johnson (Docking, 1999, p139) argues that since the reforms of the 1980s 'the teacher, whether a seasoned head or a new entrant to the profession, is now to be seen not solely as a teacher, but as a proactive manager of resources. The era of the teacher-manager has arrived.' This book and your role as a subject leader are part of this trend. Indeed, 10 or 15 years ago there would have been very few educational texts dedicated to middle management. It could be argued, though, that the role of the teacher/manager is not a novelty. Teachers have always had to manage resources carefully. The value-for-money and market-led philosophies of the late 1980s and early 1990s have developed into the school improvement and effectiveness framework of the post-1997 era.

The school improvement discourse runs all the way through the *Standards for Subject Leaders*. We are told that 'effective leadership results in... pupils who show sustained improvement in the subject knowledge, understanding and skills in relation to prior attachment' (p5). The idea that effective subject leadership results in effective pupil learning is actually very radical. Even the voices of the so-called New Right in the late 1980s would have been wary of directly attributing the complex and nebulous process of learning to something as apparently simple as good management.

Subject leaders have become accountable for the results of students within that subject. If they are the leaders of core subjects in primary schools or any examinable subject in a secondary school those results will be published and made accessible to the public. The introduction of Ofsted, a non-ministerial government agency set up as a result of the 1992 Education Act, has meant that subject leaders are always accountable to external scrutiny. Ofsted's main focus in an inspection is teaching and learning and subject leaders should certainly expect to be observed as frequently as members of their team. Time will also be given for the inspectors to interview subject leaders about their subject areas. Subject leaders must target-set for teachers and pupils and their management of teaching and learning in this sense will form an important part of the inspection. This accountability has been compounded by the introduction in 1998 of performance management.

2.4 Professional development and the new professionalism

Kenneth Baker introduced in-service training (Inset) days. These were five non-teaching days dedicated to ongoing training of teachers. The use of the word 'training' as opposed to 'development' is significant because the concept of professional development promoted by Baker and the Conservative government was one of 'one-off' training events which were directly linked to particular (often centrally decided) objectives, such as computer skills. This way of working has not disappeared. The idea of 'going on a course' for a day is still prevalent in staff rooms and you will hear colleagues talking about professional development in these terms. The *Standards*, however, adhere to a more sophisticated and ongoing view of professional development. Government pressure has shaped policy considerably. CPD, for example, is now regarded as an entitlement rather than a luxury and subject leaders may be performance managers as well as subject to performance management themselves. In this way the *Standards* can be used to audit, assess, guide and set targets, etc.

In the first chapter we examined the way that the *Standards* emerged into a complex situation regarding national education policy. They really were the first attempt by a government to structure progression for teachers' careers. Before the *Standards* were established there had never been a strategic, step-by-step career structure for teachers. Promotion had tended to happen in a fairly ad-hoc way according to the inclination of teachers to seek it and of headteachers and governing bodies to create posts. Work on teachers' professional biographies has shown that a variety of reasons spur teachers on to seek promotion and that personal and professional factors are not mutually exclusive.

In terms of career development the subject leader has a list of *Standards* to describe the qualities involved in his or her professional role. These *Standards* may be used by subject leaders to audit and chart their own professional development. They may also be used by stakeholders and line managers to reflect on this development. At the time of writing, however, they cannot be used for disciplinary or inspection purposes. The national strategy for continuing professional development has made a transparent career path with clearly defined steps towards headship for teachers. The *Standards for Subject Leadership* are an important part of this career ladder. The NCSL and GTC are also developing frameworks for career progression. The establishment of the GTC has meant that it also has a strategy of CPD with its own philosophy and the introduction of the threshold level, performance management (appraisal) review cycle and appraising colleagues has firmly linked career development with professional learning.

2.5 Inclusion and race relations

There has been, and there is still ongoing, a significant shift towards the inclusion agenda. Schools have a responsibility to provide a broad and balanced curriculum for all pupils. There are three principal aims for inclusion and they are:

- setting suitable learning challenges
- responding to pupils' diverse learning needs
- overcoming potential barriers to learning and assessment for individuals and groups of pupils including:
  - pupils with special educational needs and additional educational needs
  - pupils with all kinds of disabilities
  - pupils who are learning English as an additional language (EAL).

Some schools may choose to combine their race equality policy with other policies such as the general equal opportunities policy or the general diversity policy. Where this happens the race equality aspect of the wider policy should be easily identifiable and accessible.

Any school race equality policy will include a section on the curriculum, teaching and learning and should also involve a section on language and cultural needs. This means that each subject leader should think about the implications of the Race Relations Amendment Act 2000 in their subject area. The CfRE booklet (2002) includes useful advice on how the race equality policy should be assessed. It highlights the need for information on outcomes, needs and entitlements for pupils, parents, guardians and staff (p16). Use of attainment data will obviously play a key role in this information as will less formal data gathered from talking to parents, students and teachers. As a subject leader, therefore, you will be directly involved in the implementation of the Amendment Act.

At a whole-school level there will also be a need for ongoing monitoring of practice and collection of data such as exclusion rates, incidences of racial harassment and bullying, curriculum and teaching, punishment and rewards, support, advice and guidance and parents' and guardians' involvement in the school (p18).

2.6 Government policy and the subject leader

The history of the interchange between politics and education is a long and fraught one. The Thatcher, Major and Blair governments have taken various viewpoints on education but we can trace a trajectory towards managerialism and accountability that runs through them all.

What is often missed in discussions about the content of particular policies is that the vastly differing and complex school cultures mean that the written policy as it emanates from Whitehall is not the same as the perceived policy as it arrives in school. It could be argued that major policy documents (such as the national curriculum) are recreated and re-presented rather than implemented in schools. This is not to say that teachers have total autonomy when it comes to policy implementation but it does mean that we cannot assume that implementation is either uniform or as the government intended. Governments soon realised that there was a need to measure impact and accountability.

As Rawlings has pointed out (2001, p9), 1988 was a significant point in the history of teaching. Until 1988 many forces had played a part in shaping the school curriculum. Some were academic, some were spawned by general changes in people's lives such as the increasing influence of the media. But since 1988 the singular shaping force on the content of the school curriculum has been central government. Before then teachers could exercise political influence over the curriculum. Discontent with this situation and other aspects of state education led to the 'Black Papers' which articulated the growing feeling that standards in state education were dropping. The negativity came to a head with the Ruskin College speech made by Callaghan in 1976 in which he articulated many of the concerns about state-run education that had been a feature of both left- and right-wing perspectives in the preceding years. The trajectory towards state intervention in the business of the classroom can therefore be traced further back than 1988 and it continues now.

It could be argued that New Labour continues to take a restrictive view of education despite its rhetoric of professionalism. Indeed, there is little evidence of a clear understanding of teaching and learning in recent policy documents but instead there is a great deal of evidence of a simplistic importation of management models which are built on a low trust of the profession.

The various policy interventions described above represent significant changes in the professional lives of teachers. The effects of the management of change have been written about at length. Notably, in his book *The New Meaning of Educational Change* (1991) Michael Fullan makes the point that the visceral human responses to change should not be ignored but that they frequently are by those imposing the changes (p31). Indeed, an understanding of the psychological impact of change is almost never included in policy documents. He makes the point that it is not possible to overestimate the complexity of the change process, arguing (p95) that 'Commitment to what should be changed often varies inversely with knowledge about how to work through a process of change' – and that this epitomises the way that developments have felt to teachers since the mid-1980s.

2.7 Performance management and value added data

- Schools are now required to set targets for the percentage of pupils achieving levels in English, maths and science.
- A framework of professional development now shapes the progression of the careers of teachers.
- NQTs may be 'tutored' by subject leaders and they need to fulfil the standards for newly qualified teachers. They also have certain rights (to time and support, for example).

Rawlings (2001, p137) has pointed to the very mixed philosophical bases of New Labour's educational policies. Targets, performance indicators and the basic skills programmes represent a continuation of the right-wing policies of the previous Conservative government. Citizenship, PSHE and inclusion, however, borrow from more left-wing origins. The application of performance management indicators to the public sector is rooted in the thinking about education of the late 1980s but it started in earnest after the election of New Labour in 1997.

Task 5 Tracking government policy

TEAM TASK

Ask each member of your team to trace the representation of a current area of policy in the media for a half-term period. Examples are:

- the tensions between LEA and central government
- the examination agenda (at all levels)
- the 'basic skills' agenda (including the national strategies)
- the way that the 'teaching profession' is referred to by ministers
- inspection and accountability issues.

You may want to add others depending on your own specific context. Then use part of a staff meeting to discuss your findings. The purpose is to help the team to understand and interact with the wider policy agenda. This can help you move from a position of always being last on the list of the 'receiving end' of macro policy to a position where you and your team can at least perceive patterns in policy and anticipate developments.

As with other team tasks in this book, the aim is to incrementally move the team from a passive relationship with policy to an active one. You may meet resistance to some of these activities. Below are some ways that you might counter this resistance.

Task 6 Overcoming resistance to engagement with policy

Ask members of your team to consider the following statements and counter arguments.

Resistance voiced	Counter argument
Why are we wasting time on this? Can't we get on with more practical issues?	I think this is important. I want us to be able to take an informed approach to our own policy-writing and it will not be possible if we create policies in isolation. Also I am interested in the professional stances we take in relation to these policies.
What's the point in even discussing government policy – they'll do what they want anyway!	They say that they are in the middle of a consultation process on (x). We ought to take part in that exercise, no matter how cynical we are about how seriously our points are taken. Even if there is a concerted governmental 'push' on some of these issues, it is important that we see how they fit into the bigger picture. We have a vision for where we want this subject to go and we can be more empowered in exercising this vision if we are not placed in a passive, knee-jerk relationship with anything that comes our way.
I didn't have time to look in the newspapers. I was too busy marking.	We are professionals, not technicists. I believe that very strongly. If we want to work as professionals then we must find ways of reflecting on our practice and discussing the bigger picture. Should we take time as a team to explore new ways of incorporating a wider variety of assessment methods into our practice so that you don't have to mark every waking hour?
What has LEA funding (or equivalent) got to do with me?	A lot. You want to work in a stimulating environment, don't you? The departmental/school funding is linked directly to these bigger issues.

2.8 Operational

■ Fullan argues (1991, p130) that 'Change is a process not an event'. The more collegiality that you as a subject leader can engender, the less you will feel isolated.

■ Develop networks and cultivate personal contact.

■ Develop an underlying set of principles and philosophy against which to measure change.

■ Accept that change is inevitable.

2.9 Summary

■ The policy changes of the last few years have been far-reaching and have changed the professional identities and practices of teachers considerably.

■ Many of these changes have been brought in without evidence of a great deal of understanding on the part of the policymakers about the psychological needs of those 'at the sharp end' of the change implementation process.

■ Of all the changes since 1988 the introduction of the national curriculum as part of the 1988 Education Reform Act remains the policy that has the greatest impact on the role of the subject leader.

■ The first term of the Labour government saw the introduction of the national strategy for CPD. As we have seen, this denoted more structure to a teacher's career progression than had ever been in place before. As a result, the *Standards for Subject Leaders* are intended to form part of a continuum of progression towards the standards for headteachers. On closer analysis it appears that the vocabulary and sentiments embedded in the standards for headteachers are also to be found in all the other standards representing leadership posts in the pack. They are all derived from the same school improvement and effectiveness origins.

■ All the indications suggest that the wider political agenda of school improvement, leadership and accountability are here to stay for the subject leader. In his first speech as Secretary of State for Education, Charles Clarke (2002, Oxford speech) continued to use the language of the Standards and Effectiveness Unit – improvement, leadership and performance. The old-style head of department, it seems, is now just a memory. At least in the national policymaker's view, the new-style subject leader is here to stay.

■ There is a counter-argument, though, and we will turn to it again in chapter 10. Some feel school improvement has had its day and that transformation is now a buzz-word, requiring creative leadership. According to this perspective, subject leaders may need to redefine what is learnt, and how the learning happens (West Burnham, 2003) and schools can only be so good before they start to redefine what constitutes 'good'. Standards may only need maintaining but the by-products of learning (social participation, creativity) might get better, according to this theory.

Policies relating to the delivery of the subject and the curriculum

Chapter 3

Objectives

By the end of this chapter you will have examined the policies that currently have a direct impact on the content of the curriculum and subject delivery. These concern:

- the literacy and numeracy strategies and the national key stage 3 strategy

- citizenship

- culture and creativity

- key skills and the 14-19 agenda

- provision for gifted and talented pupils

- ICT.

The mandatory status of these policies varies but in general each subject leader will have some responsibility to deliver the policy within the confines of the subject and by contributing to the curriculum as a whole. The tasks in this chapter are linked to particular policies. They are intended to be used as starting-points for discussions in team meetings.

3.1 Regulatory

The *Standards for Subject Leaders* (TTA, 1998) have much to say about the implications of particular policies for the work of subject leaders. Specifically, they look at:

- the need for subject leaders to have knowledge and understanding of any statutory curriculum requirements for the subject and the requirements for assessment, recording and reporting of pupils' attainment and progress (3c, p6)

- how to develop pupils' literacy, numeracy and ICT skills through the subject (3g, p6)

- the current use and future potential of ICT to aid teaching and learning of the subject (3k, p6)

- the implications of information and guidance documents from LEAs, the DfES and other national bodies and associations (3m, p6)

- how to ensure effective development of pupils' literacy, numeracy and information technology skills through the subject (biv, p11)

- how to ensure that teachers of a subject are aware of its contribution to pupils' understanding of the duties, opportunities, responsibilities and rights of citizens (bx, p11).

It can be seen from these *Standards* that although some policy initiatives are explicitly mentioned (literacy, numeracy and ICT), the TTA is aware that education policy-making is in a continual state of development, hence the catch-all standard (3m) which stipulates that subject leaders should make appropriate use of guidance documents from central and local government. Since the *Standards* were written in 1998 some of the policies examined in this chapter have been developed. These include citizenship, provision for gifted and talented pupils, the emphasis on culture and creativity encapsulated in the document *All Our Futures* (DfEE, 1999) and the significant and far-reaching changes that have had an impact on secondary schoolteachers as part of the revised provision for pupils aged 14–19. Underpinning this section is the assumption that the policy developments implemented since 1998 are part of the statutory duty of the subject leader's role, even though they are not mentioned directly, because of the all-encompassing standard about understanding and implementing policy guidance documents that emanate from central government.

Consideration of the effect of these policies when regarded as a whole is given below. In the following section on the operational implications of the policies, a more detailed analysis of the content of each policy is given, along with some guidelines about how subject leaders can work within the wider political context.

3.2　Discussion

The policies examined in this chapter form the specifics of the New Labour education policy since the beginning of its first term in 1997. They can loosely be grouped together because they all relate to the management of learning. Possibly the strategy with the most far-reaching effect on you – whether you work in a primary or secondary school – is the emphasis on literacy and numeracy and its manifestation in the eponymous strategies and extension in the secondary school: the national strategy for key stage 3. This intervention has the biggest impact because not only is it cross-curricular (in primary schools subject leaders of subjects other than literacy and numeracy will feel its impact on their subjects in the compromises made to the timetable for it) but it is intensely pedagogical. The strategy is concerned not only with what is taught but also how it is taught. It represents a major development in the history of state intervention in the ways that schools are run.

The Conservative government was thought by some to be radically right-wing in the late 1980s when it introduced a national curriculum, the content of which was decided centrally. A decade on, the New Labour government was deciding not only the content of the subjects that used to be known as maths and English but also the methods that teachers should adopt in their teaching of those subjects. The early version of the national literacy strategy was even accompanied by a structure of an hour which could be used as a basis for every lesson plan. To this extent, the major sweep of policies introduced by the New Labour government in its first term can never be dismissed as marginal; they affect all teachers.

Standards and effectiveness

For teachers this has had a major impact on how we think about professionalism. Hoyle (1995) categorises professionals into two groups: the **restricted** professionals, who are highly competent and who embody the popular image of professionalism but who are compliant with their managers and their demands; and the second group, the **extended** professionals, who are all of the above but who define their own parameters in their work. It is difficult for teachers to become extended professionals if the government decides not only what is taught but the nature of the teaching and learning experience. The accompanying emphasis on the role of the subject leader and the accountability of middle management has made the implementation of these changes compulsory. Subject leaders need to work hard to maintain a sense of shared philosophy for a subject while at the same time incorporating the policy documents into the work of the subject team.

It is notable that many of these policies have originated from the Standards and Effectiveness Unit within the Department for Education. This unit was concerned mainly in the first term of the New Labour government with overall standards in the education system. It concerned itself with the reasons why schools failed and aimed to get all schools to learn from the successful ones. In the second term, however, the attention of the unit was turned to the nature of what is taught in schools. This is mainly demonstrated by the national strategy for key stage 3.

High-quality teaching and learning as the main focus for a school's entire activities is a desirable feature of both school effectiveness (Sammons *et al*, 1995) and school improvement (Hargreaves and Hopkins, 1993). The whole experience of leadership must, it is argued, always conspire to enhance the learning experience for the pupils. The emphasis that school improvement places on teaching and learning and the potential of the teaching professional to make a difference to the lives of pupils could be regarded as central to the role of the subject leader, as set out in the *Standards for Subject Leaders*, as well as to the national strategy for key stage 3. Interestingly the second slide in the 'Subject leadership at Key Stage 3' section of the *'Briefing Pack for School Strategy Managers: subject leader development programme'* combines the *Standards* and the strategy immediately (p5). It goes on to say that the core roles for subject leaders are:
- making judgments about standards of pupils' achievement
- evaluating teaching and learning and setting priorities for improvement
- leading sustainable improvement by identifying targets for improvement, by developing and leading strategies to achieve these targets and by quality-assuring the curriculum (p2).

Whether or not there is a consistent New Labour ideology relating to education is difficult to say. The policies set out above are born out of a variety of doctrinal bases. The dominant idea of education servicing economic growth, which characterised Tory education policy, is still evident in the massive governmental commitment to the strategies. The functional nature of literacy and numeracy and ICT has much in common with what might be described as the *adult needs* view of the curriculum. The perceived needs of employers are the incentive for the strategies, at least in part, and this follows on from the push towards technical and vocational education in the 1980s.

There is also, though, an identifiable train of thought which is about democracy and active citizenship in these policies which seems to be genuine. The drive for literacy, as well as the citizenship initiative, is characterised by references to the impact of education on society in general. The creation of a healthy, active democracy through education certainly seems to be an emerging and enduring characteristic of the policies created in the first term of New Labour's governance. How far this extends in practice, though, is debatable. Presumably the demonstration of active citizenship by thousands of school pupils who took to the streets in opposition to the proposed war against Iraq in February 2003 was not greeted by cheers at the DfES as the best proof that the citizenship curriculum had worked.

New Labour, new vision?

As the first secretary of state for education in the New Labour government, David Blunkett focused on inclusion and raising standards. Estelle Morris took this further with the introduction of the new professional development framework which included plans for an unprecedented increase in powers and responsibility for learning support assistants. In his first speech as the new education secretary in 2002 Charles Clarke drew attention to the new professionalism which would have an impact on teachers and the expansion of the teaching profession to include teaching assistants who could be trained to a level high enough to allow them to take some of the pressure away from teachers.

Although some ideological consistency can be found in the policies, there are also significant contradictions. The need for intellectual risk-taking and licence to make mistakes, as made concrete in the *All Our Futures* (DfEE, 1999) document, directly contradicts the testing agenda embedded in the national curriculum and baseline assessments, for example. Writing about the numeracy strategy in particular, Brown and MacNamara (2001, p52) argue that 'Current government policies aimed at raising standards in primary schools have been experienced by many primary teachers in terms of initiative overload'. This fact cannot be separated from the content of the policies. All real change involves loss, anxiety and struggle. These are unpleasant and wearing emotions in oneself and in others. If you are really to take a genuine leadership role regarding these policies you must recognise that the management of change will be ongoing and will not stop once the policy has been 'implemented'.

We need to ask whether the current emphasis on teachers teaching according to particular policies is, in fact, a governmental tool which has been designed to enforce conformity.

3.3 Operational

We will now examine the practice implications for you of the following policies:
- literacy, numeracy and the national strategy for key stage 3
- citizenship
- culture and creativity
- key skills
- gifted and talented pupils
- ICT.

The literacy and numeracy strategies and the national strategy for key stage 3

The national strategies for literacy and numeracy have been followed in secondary schools by the introduction of the national strategy for key stage 3. It is intended to address the perceived dip in achievement and attainment in the transition between key stages 2 and 3. Central to its design is the insistence that secondary schoolteachers should build on the work that has gone on in key stage 2.

The restructuring of the content of the curriculum that followed the 1988 Education Reform Act has been matched by the incremental but equally trenchant changes to the curriculum in primary schools, and more recently at key stage 3, that have been brought about by the national strategy and the placing of literacy, numeracy and science at the centre of the primary curriculum. The national strategy for key stage 3 comprises several strands – English and literacy; maths and numeracy; science; foundation subjects and ICT; and soon to be included are behaviour and attendance. The national strategy for key stage 3 is the most important of the policies because in a sense it supersedes and incorporates all of the others. All strands promote the following:

- high expectations
- clear objectives
- medium- and short-term planning
- structured lessons
- challenging and engaging activities and tasks
- manageable differentiation
- interactive teaching
- effective questioning
- time for pupils to reflect.

There are some guidelines about the practical considerations concerning the delivery of the strategy. For example, for ICT 'the recommendation of the strategy is that schools provide one hour per week of discrete teaching of ICT'. Schools are encouraged to audit ICT provision at key stage 3 and subject leaders should liaise with the ICT coordinator about schemes of work. In terms of the overall management of the strategy, senior managers tend to take responsibility for one or two subjects.

Although the strategy is apparently voluntary, few schools are sufficiently intrepid to ignore it. The key stage 3 strategy is housed in the Standards and Effectiveness Unit and as a result the school improvement discourse runs all the way through the strategy. Soon after taking office as education secretary David Blunkett announced that primary schools need no longer teach the full programmes of study in the non-core subjects of art, D and T, geography, history, music and PE in order to make more room for literacy and numeracy. A dedicated folder is available from the DfES which explains in detail what the expectations of subject leaders are and this would be a useful document for subject leaders to consult.

Task 7	Literacy and numeracy

TEAM TASK
What does your subject do to promote literacy and numeracy? How do you and your subject team promote literacy and numeracy? Discuss as a group first and then broaden the discussion to include the school's literacy strategy coordinator.

Citizenship

The citizenship curriculum was implemented in 2002. It is a means of teaching anti-racist education, democracy and other issues. You will have to consider how you incorporate this curriculum into your own subject area and this policy will be dealt with in more detail in the next chapter.

Task 8	Citizenship and the subject leader

TEAM TASK

Take the following ideas from the citizenship curriculum and map them against your schemes of work:

- the environment and sustainable development
- human rights
- democracy.

The purpose of citizenship education is to educate students about democracy and its constituent parts and to develop the knowledge, skills and values necessary in order to participate in a democracy. It consists of learning about social and moral responsibility; community involvement and political literacy.

Since September 2002, citizenship has been a national curriculum subject. At key stages 3 and 4 a 'separate articulation of citizenship is essential' but there can also be a cross-curricular element to its delivery while it is part of the PSHE and citizenship framework in primary schools. At key stages 1 and 2 schools must report pupils' progress to parents. At key stage 2, there is teacher assessment of pupils' progress in the citizenship curriculum and although at key stage 4 there are no formal arrangements, schools can choose to run a GCSE in citizenship.

Education is never neutral. Subject leaders should therefore instigate and facilitate discussions with members of their team in order to identify and reduce evidence of bias in teaching and teaching plans. The obvious overlap with citizenship is with the subjects of English, geography, history, PSHE and RE, but there is potential to combine it with all other subjects in the curriculum. Field (2004) has written in detail about the contradictions and benefits involved in cross-curricular citizenship teaching.

As subject leader, you could access the curriculum for citizenship education with the aim of promoting concordance with it. You should also scan and audit your team's own schemes of work and departmental policies for evidence of citizenship. There are, however, no level descriptors for the citizenship curriculum.

Although there are no level descriptors, it is incumbent on subject leaders to identify aspects of the citizenship curriculum that can be addressed by their subject area and to highlight links. This means examining and auditing schemes of work and monitoring provision.

Other issues associated with citizenship are more complex. Subject leaders will need to think about the extent to which teachers practice what they preach. In other words, subject leaders may have to support teachers in their reflections on how appropriate a didactic, autocratic teaching style is in a lesson on democracy and freedom of speech. At a more profound level, the teaching and learning of the subject needs to be underpinned by explicit values which adhere to those taught.

Culture and creativity

In 1999 the DfEE produced the document *All Our Futures*. In essence it recommends creative teaching and learning and it encourages teachers to recognise that all children have a wide range of abilities. It also emphasises the importance of broader aspects of creativity in the curriculum as a direct response to the changing workplace.

Creativity can be defined as a combination of the following four elements: value, imagination, originality and purpose. In the *All Our Futures* document, creativity is also linked to thinking skills. Schools can choose to implement the creativity and thinking skills initiative across the curriculum or to limit its application to two or three subjects.

It could be argued that one of the effects of the national strategy, dealt with earlier in this chapter, has been to lessen the potential of implementing the suggestions made in the *All Our Futures* document. The national strategy and the aforementioned document come from different and at times contradictory bases. The utilitarian, 'adult skills' and employability agenda of the former undermines the more liberal tone of the latter, which stresses personal development (albeit in line with skills that are required by the workplace). There are no extra requirements made of teachers or subject leaders.

It is, however, your responsibility to ensure that the curriculum allows for different ways of learning and for creative teaching and learning to take place. This should be part of the natural differentiation process at the planning stage. Creative teaching can get in the way of creative learning, though a better term is teaching for creativity. This prevents teachers dominating the learning experience with virtuoso performances. Central to the teaching should be the commitment to the pupils' need to be creative!

You should consider the values which their subject represents and whether it fits in with the enduring values and ethos of the school. Subject leaders should seek to incorporate the professional knowledge available on thinking skills and multiple intelligences – for example, Gardner (1983) and Goleman (1996) – when planning for the teaching in their subject and this awareness should ideally run through all policies and associated documentation. As with other aspects of the management of policies, they should also be monitored.

Task 9	Learning styles and thinking skills

TEAM TASK

Audit your schemes of work. What do they do to promote a variety of learning styles and thinking skills? Do they need to be adapted to include more dynamic approaches?

Key skills 14–19

At the time of writing consultation is ongoing about the green paper *14–19 Extending Opportunities, Raising Standards*. It states that the vision is to 'broaden the skills acquired by all young people to improve their employability, bridge the skills gap identified by employers and overcome social exclusion'. The government wants to see key skills as a priority and wants to move into a position where they are a normal part of everyone's post-16 qualification.

Direct links are made between learning and the sorts of skills that employers are assumed to need. These are:
- communication
- application of number
- ICT
- working with others
- improving own learning and performance
- problem-solving.

The main thrust behind the key skills agenda is about employability and industrial competitiveness. Links can be found with the key stage 3 strategy in that it is driven by the skills apparently most favoured by employers. Both strategies are part of a view of education that is both utilitarian and committed to liberating individuals from poverty and unemployment.

Task 10	Cross-phase work

TEAM TASK

Discuss the following:

How much do you as a team know about learning development beyond the immediate key stage with which you work? How much do you think about preparing students for vocational learning? How much attention do you pay to pupil data from the previous key stage of education in your subject?

Gifted and talented pupils

Schools are now required to identify the 'top' 10% of their pupils. Each school should have a policy on how it works with gifted and talented pupils. Ideas for subject-specific policies for subject leaders may be found at the website www.nc.uk.net/gt/subjects/monitoring

Whole-school policies on gifted and talented pupils should include:
- policy rationale and aims
- definitions
- identification
- provision
- organisational issues
- transfer and transition
- resources
- monitoring and evaluation.

Task 11	Gifted and talented pupils

TEAM TASK

As a subject team, define what constitutes talented pupils in your subject area. What can you do to extend these pupils and to raise the achievement of other pupils as well?

Ofsted will look at how the school identifies gifted and talented students; the level of teachers' awareness of pupils' needs; the willingness of teachers to adapt and adjust their teaching to rapid development; the school's strategies to involve all teachers in the provision of subject support; and how the school uses the sources of support.

Gifted pupils are those who have abilities in one or more subjects in the statutory school curriculum other than art and design, music and PE. Talented pupils are those who have abilities in art and design, music, PE, sports or the performing arts such as dance and drama.

At subject level secondary schools should ensure consistency across departments in their provision for gifted and talented pupils. Three ways of achieving these aims are through acceleration, extension and enrichment.

ICT

ICT is a statutory part of the national curriculum, not only for students in school but also as part of initial teacher education. A good deal of public money has been poured into increasing ICT provision in schools and the interest in e-learning is growing. Hughes (2004) has written about the way that ICT can liberate teachers' practice. Where technology leads pedagogy follows, or at least that has been the case for the past two decades when technology has grown in its presence in the education system. Ideally there should be as much thought and professional consideration about how to teach with information technology as there is about any other pedagogical tool. The challenge for subject leaders is how to move away from the vague notion that ICT is *a good thing* to a meaningful way of using it to genuinely enhance learning. In your subject, in other words, you need to move away from the situation where ICT is used for the sake of it to one where ICT is used because it fulfils a particular learning need better than any other method.

ICT is always playing a dual role in the curriculum; on the one hand, as we have said, it is enhancing teaching and learning about other subjects. On the other, though, it is assumed that students are simultaneously developing their ICT skills. This is the area where the perceived problems often lie because many of the young people being taught have a higher level of ICT confidence and competence than the teachers who teach them. One of the primary tasks for the subject leader, then, is to ensure that the teachers of the subject have ongoing access to training opportunities and a secure environment in which to discuss their developing knowledge (or lack of it!). As time goes on this will become a diminishing problem as all student teachers now have to demonstrate ICT competence in order to gain Qualified Teacher Status. National curriculum documentation also provides detailed suggestions as to when ICT can be

Task 12 **ICT and administration**

INDIVIDUAL TASK

Make a list of the administrative tasks that you typically undertake in a single day. Now divide them into tasks that require a face-to-face element and those that do not.

Face-to-face required	Face-to-face not required

Consider the specific requirements of ICT when used in the classroom and think about ways of facilitating high-quality use of ICT for your team.

TEAM TASK

Plot the results of the questions in the individual task (above) onto a chart. As a group discuss how well this could be developed by more extensive use of ICT.

used in subject areas and there are a number of online sources of support for teachers in their work with ICT at a variety of levels. These include the National Grid for Learning (www.ngfl.gov.uk), the Virtual Teachers Centre (www.forum.ngfl.gov.uk) and the British Educational Communications and Technology Agency (www.becta.org.uk).

Where teachers have access to computers they can play an enormously time-saving role in the bureaucracy of the schoolday. Email and assessment data handling are examples of this.

The increased emphasis on the collection of value added data in the classroom has also meant that ICT has a valuable role to play – ie, ICT for administration and management purposes as well as learning.

3.4 Summary

- Check DfES and QCA guidelines for how these policies should be implemented in your own subject area. The Gifted and Talented website (www.teachernet.gov.uk) and the national strategy for key stage 3 websites both have particular advice for subject areas.
- Work with school managers to bring subject documentation and teaching into line with whole-school policies.
- The philosophy of the subject among the subject team should be firm and government initiatives should, as far as possible, be assessed within that context.
- There should be as much thought about why ICT is to be used as about how it is used.

Policy, practice and vision

Chapter 4

Objectives

By the end of this chapter you will have:

- established what vision is and started to explore why vision is regarded as important

- considered how vision fits in with other procedures and documents in a school

- considered the characteristics of school cultures where policies and vision are understood and shared.

4.1 Regulatory

There are two types of internal policy documents: those required by government agencies and the senior management team, and those designed by the subject team because they enhance good practice. Good practice and inherited cultural norms also mean that a number of other documents and plans generally exist as well in a school. These external and internal requirements differ in their demands for the format and the content of such documents but in general both sets of documents fit into the following hierarchy:

- vision
- mission
- strategic plan
- school development plan
- policies
- annual review
- pegular review and adjustment
- post-Ofsted plan
- action plans.

(Adapted from Field *et al*, 2001, p163)

The overarching nature of the school development plan and any strategic planning that accompanies it will inform the policy construction at subject team level. There is, therefore, something of a balancing act necessary if you are to retain the integrity of your own leadership and the philosophy of the team without compromising the goals and vision of the senior management team.

The *Standards for Subject Leaders* (TTA, 1998) clearly state that 'The effectiveness of the subject leader will depend on... the way in which decisions, policies and practices are communicated and implemented throughout the school' (p9, section 5). There is an acknowledgment here that you are not completely autonomous – that there is a level of dependency on the overall school culture and the effectiveness of the head. That said, you do need to take responsibility for your own subject area.

The section in the *Standards* on p10 is concerned with 'strategic direction and development of the subject'. It states that 'within the context of the school's aims and policies, subject leaders develop and implement subject policies, plans, targets and practices'. This includes subject policies which:

- reflect high achievement, effective learning and teaching
- reflect subject leaders' understanding of how the subject contributes to the pupils' moral, cultural, mental and physical development (iii).

As for the process of creating the policies, the *Standards* state that subject leaders need to establish, with the involvement of relevant staff, short-, medium- and long-term plans which contribute to whole-school aims, policies and practice on:

- behaviour, discipline, bullying and racial harassment.

It also suggests that these policies are to be understood by all those involved in putting plans into practice.

Clearly it is not enough that the policies are created and developed. There must be clear evidence of leadership in the creation process as well as the enduring monitoring of those policies. Policies are part of the quality assurance procedure because they represent the realisation of ideas, and also provide criteria against which participants can measure success. They may be prescriptive as well as descriptive. A good policy contains:

- the organisation's mission
- a description of the management system and staff responsibilities
- a description of quality assurance procedures, functions and review procedures.

4.2 Discussion

Managing the change process

Before we examine the competing theories relating to policy-writing it is worth pausing to reflect on what effect the constant state of planning and improvement has on people. Field *et al* (2000, p113) point out that for many, living in a 'could do better' world is a normal state. This does not just apply to teachers – one of the effects of living in a consumerist, capitalist society is that we all are fed a diet of what we lack – be it a beautiful face or a new car – by an army of advertisers and the media. Teachers have a double bind because we are prey not only to the ravages of the accountability culture but also the philanthropic impetus that leads many to teaching in the first place. This can work against us as all the ills of society are often landed at our door. It is important that you bear this in mind and emphasise what the strengths of the team are before you begin the strategic planning process and the changes that it will inevitably bring. Some models of team dynamics attribute different roles to different team members, for example, and suggest that there are not ideal types of people to have in a team but rather the richer the mixture the better.

No amount of policy-writing will be of any use if it does not lead to a change in practice. As we have said, all change is in some way traumatic and a wise subject leader anticipates and knows how to manage negative reactions to change in him/herself as well as in others. There are various interpretations of how humans react to change, but in its simplest form change incurs negativity before positive results can be experienced. Where ownership of the impetus and nature of this change is shared, the negative feelings can also be shared and supported.

Sometimes, though, a subject leader will need to simply impose change. Goddard and Leask (1992, pp185-190) have identified various stages of the change process. They identify the following:

- the reactive phase, in which colleagues may resist change
- the transition phase, in which change is gradually accepted
- the significant level of development work, in which staff recognise the value of the process
- the collaborative phase, in which staff begin to work with representatives outside the team
- the evaluation stage, in which the policies are reviewed against the initial reasons for creating them
- the strategic planning in which real change and development in the future is set down.

Change may be improvement (which is continual change that builds on the past and is relatively slow) or it could be incremental (doing something new) or revolutionary (doing something completely new) (Field *et al*, 2000, p126). Participating in the change process means that people are likely to go through stages of denial, resistance, exploration and finally commitment. Morale is likely to dip in the beginning and middle stages of change implementation and you will need to compensate for this in your leadership style.

It is important to remember that the process is so complex when embarking on a new initiative. Ideally any policy-writing should begin with a strategic plan and link to the vision which is articulated in the mission statement. The mission states the purpose and the vision describes what the provision looks like. Together they allow these ideas to be interpreted as real plans. Ideally these plans should be the tangible documents that reflect the values articulated in the grander vision and the overarching mission statement.

School development plans serve internal and external purposes. Internally they show staff where they are going and externally they are documents available to governors, inspectors and other stakeholders. The vision should feed into a strategic plan. This is the subject leader's own plan for how work within the department or subject area could be managed. It is the directional framework within which the operational activities of the subject team can take place. There should be a shared and coherent plan about what needs to change. In reality, though, what often happens is that there is an external or internal demand for a policy which is then hastily created without the deep-level thinking or soul-searching that is necessary for a genuine implementation of whole-school aims and strategic goals.

Field *et al* (2000, p165) argue that 'By building a policy together, defining the purpose and methods, the subject leader has an opportunity to engage in team-building exercises. The process of policy-writing enables a clear subject team identity to be built through the sharing of collective vision, which when implemented will permeate all teachers' work.'

Harris (1999, p35) also points out that 'the starting point for high achievement within any subject area is good curriculum planning. Effective planning is a vital component of the successful department. The right planning process will not only contribute to quality assurance but can offer a way of managing change.'

4.3   Operational

William Blake wrote that 'Vision or Imagination is a representation of what/Eternally Exists, Really and Unchangeably' (*A Vision of the Last Judgment*, 1810). It is your challenge to make the vision real. The implementation of the vision is often presented as a key feature of leadership. It is worth considering whether it is also considered a key feature of management because the two terms – management and leadership – do not describe two groups of people: the leaders manage and the managers, hopefully, lead. We talk about subject leadership, for example, but generally the term subject leaders is not common – we still use the traditional term 'senior management team' by and large.

It is worth adding a word of caution here. Visions can be worthless if they are not accompanied by action. A common question asked by inspectors is: what is the school's mission statement? In schools where the mission statement is no more than a collection of words on a wall plaque, there is no shared understanding and the so-called vision is worthless because it does not drive the more detailed policy-writing and consequent actions of the school. Where a vision is shared, though, the school development plan can prioritise the school's activities in the political framework. Fleming (2000, p60) argues that 'having a shared goal is the first thing that distinguishes groups from teams. That is why it is so important that the team leader has a clear sense of direction.'

Task 13	Influences on your vision of the subject

INDIVIDUAL TASK

Write down the names of three individuals whom you admire connected to your subject. These might be famous people like athletes or scientists but they might also be people pertinent to your own life – such as a really inspirational teacher or a relative connected to the subject. Now for each one write down what it is that they represent about the subject that appeals to you. This will help you to articulate what the subject really means to you and lay the foundations for a more detailed elaboration of your ideas in the vision for the subject as you develop it with your team (see below).

Senior management will be required to write the school development plan and the post-Ofsted action plan. Of these, the post-Ofsted action plan is the one that is most obviously required for an external audience. All schools are required to produce an action plan after an Ofsted inspection. The purpose of this is intended to be the raising of achievement in the areas for development highlighted in the report. Although a variety of things will be highlighted in the report as areas for improvement, planners should concentrate on linking their plans for improvement to the areas of teaching and learning. Teams need to subscribe to the vision and this is an aspect of effective departments which has been repeatedly identified in research (eg Harris, 1999). This vision is said to embrace an understanding of the subject and what constitutes good teaching and learning of that subject; the vision is shared and debated among members of the team and the vision has a very real impact on how teaching and learning are organised in the departments. The corollary is that a lack of vision, it is argued, is a defining feature of ineffective departments and schools.

The process of writing the whole-school development plan is probably self-explanatory. Planners (including the senior management team and other members of staff – see below) will review the existing development plan and then identify the school's strengths and weaknesses with reference to the Ofsted report. They then set a timetable and ensure that all staff are aware of their roles in its implementation. Subject leaders should expect to have an input into but not write the action plan. Where possible, it is important that subject leaders have some input into the school development plan because it will have a major impact on the content and tone of all the subject team's policies. The school development plan will, by its very nature, comply with national policy initiatives and the LEA's education development plan.

The education development plan is a three-year plan. LEAs are required by the government to create these three-year plans which will include their targets and plans for school improvement. These have to be approved by the education secretary and they must be created in consultation with schools. In reality this consultation means that performance targets must be negotiated and professional development needs will be identified. The implications for the subject leader are that needs can be communicated to the LEA and there are possibilities for networking with subject leaders in similar positions across the LEA. The emphasis on targets for pupils' performance, however, means that subject leaders will have a very important role concerning the predictions and improvements of pupil attainment.

In primary schools subject leaders will have to work within the confines of LEA-imposed targets for Level 4 attainment in core subjects. In order for any of these to be effective, an audit will need to be first carried out. Development planning is now common in schools. Research (MacGilchrist *et al*, 1995) shows that effective schools sustain collaborative cultures where planning is shared. An audit allows members of staff to assess where the school is at the present time in order to plan where the school will be in one, five or 10 years' time.

Task 14	The team's vision

TEAM TASK
- Write four statements about what your vision of the subject is.
- Now arrange the statements in descending order.
- Eliminate the bottom two.
- Now join up with everybody else's statements.
- Go through the same process again.
- Choose the top three statements.
- Finally write a paragraph that conceptualises the three statements.

It is worth stating here that all of these aspects of policy and vision appear to be very simple in the abstract. The nature of the real life of schools, however, means that in reality the subject leader exists in a messy mix of teaching, assessing, bureaucracy and team-leading, and subject policies will have to be created in this context. Some management texts seem to suggest that management is the subject leader's only responsibility and activity. This is not the case.

As Lortie (1975) has shown us, teachers constantly struggle to retain clarity in the face of several competing and contradictory constraints (or what he calls 'presses'). For example teachers' working days are defined by hundreds, if not several thousands, of interactions with students but this is coupled with relative isolation from other adults. If this is the case for classroom teachers then the demands on teachers who also have to carry out a management role make it all the more so.

One way subject leaders can look clearly at the substance of what is going on in their subject areas, without the distraction of daily events is by using the SWOT analysis technique. By drawing up a grid of the strengths, weaknesses, opportunities and threats (SWOT) the subject leader can look at the way that the subject is being taught very clearly. It is important to be as realistic as possible when completing a SWOT analysis and also to be rigorous and base judgments on hard evidence rather than impressions. This minimises the potential for future disagreement.

Task 15	Turning the vision into policy

TEAM TASK

Use the headings and questions below as a starting-point for a team discussion on how policy can reflect the vision for the subject. You may want to use large sheets of paper to write down the ideas that are generated.

- Why are we doing what we are doing?
- What would we fight to retain about our subject teaching if it came under threat?
- Where are we going?
- What developments would we implement if time and money were no object?
- What needs to change?

The key point for you as a subject leader is not to deny team members' emotional responses to change when you present them with the need for a new policy or a change of policy. Their feelings will be complicated and deep-seated and therefore very important. You will dismiss their responses at your peril. The initial negative responses to change must not only be acknowledged by the subject leader but time should be put aside to listen to these ideas. It is important to remember that whether the change is a response to an initiative imposed by government or by senior management, or whether the change has been initiated by the subject leader, the fact is that the subject leader will have had time to assimilate and consider the need for the change long before it is presented to the team. He or she will have had time to deal with the uncomfortable feelings that beset other members of the team well before they hear about many of the new ideas. Too many subject leaders do not acknowledge their own mixed responses to change and forget the time necessary to come to terms with change.

Once listened to, people tend to become more optimistic and supportive of the change process. This can only happen, though, if they feel that they have genuinely been consulted. A consultation that only pays lip service to listening to other people's ideas is not only a waste of time but it can also be negative and destructive as team members combine feelings of resentment with their already negative response to the ideas of change.

You need to remember that people adapt to change in various ways and although it is somewhat simplistic, it is helpful to think about these reactions more as a cycle or a tide than a relentless upward trajectory. The initial inquisitiveness will often be followed by denial and more systematic refusal to comply. Often these negative responses must be traversed before a team can genuinely adopt a new idea and enjoy implementing it. Ideally, you should offer support for the team members at each stage as they occur but you'll need to remember that the human response to change is highly complex. Like the tide, at times it will seem that you are really making progress, only to have your hopes dashed as team members become more negative again. We look at the complex nature of change in more detail in chapter 9.

4.4 Summary

- ■ Visions need to be shared.
- ■ The transition between the hierarchy of policies should be seamless.
- ■ Change is a complex process which elicits a range of psychological responses.

The wise subject leader does not deny these responses but allows team members to articulate their feelings and he or she supports them at the most challenging stages.

Managing up and managing down: creating policies in a complicated structure

Chapter 5

> **Objectives**
>
> By the end of this chapter you will have:
>
> - explored the contradictions and sensitivities inherent in the subject leader's 'middle management' role
>
> - examined who the 'stakeholders' are who have an impact on the middle management role
>
> - considered guidelines about how to work successfully with junior and senior members of staff.

5.1 Regulatory

The *Standards for Subject Leaders* (TTA, 1998) have the following to say about the position and role of the subject leader in the school hierarchy: 'It is important that a subject leader has an understanding of how their subject contributes to school priorities and to the overall education and achievement of all pupils'. Your understanding of effective learning needs to go beyond the boundaries of your own subject area and encompass a wider gaze.

In the skills and attributes section we are told that 'Subject leaders should be able to judge when to make decisions, when to consult with others, and when to defer to the headteacher or senior managers'.

The key areas of subject leadership are:
1) strategic direction and development of the subject
2) teaching and learning
3) leading and managing staff
4) efficient and effective deployment of staff and resources.

Within this framework we are told that 'it is assumed that the subject leader works closely with the headteacher and senior management team in each of the four key areas, and liaises with other colleagues as appropriate' (p9).

The *Standards* define the core purpose of the subject leader as providing 'leadership and direction for the subject'. The school improvement idea of leadership and the communication of a vision is therefore the TTA's starting point and this is in line with the research into school effectiveness and school improvement. The day-to-day work involved with the running of management also features prominently in the *Standards*. We are told that the subject is 'managed and organised to meet the aims and objectives of the school and the subject' (p4).

These statements demonstrate the complexity of your position. At the same time you must motivate staff within your own team as well as being accountable to senior managers. The headteacher is not the only stakeholder in the process. The governors also have responsibility for school improvement. 'While the headteacher and governors carry overall responsibility for school improvement, a subject leader has responsibility for securing high standards of teaching and learning in their subject as well as playing a major role in the development of school policy and practice' (p4).

It is the 'as well as' that makes your role so challenging. This is also demonstrated in section 2 of the *Standards*, 'the key outcomes of subject leadership'. The section on other teachers is predictably the longest but there is also a section on headteachers and senior managers who, we are told, are able to 'use information about achievements and development priorities in the subject in order to make well informed decisions and to achieve greater improvements in the whole school's development and its aims'.

Specific advice for leading and managing staff is given in section c, p11 of the *Standards*. 'Subject leaders provide to all those with involvement in the teaching or support of the subject, the support, challenge, information and development necessary to sustain motivation and secure improvement in teaching.'

Therefore, the *Standards* leave the guidelines regarding when to defer and when to delegate relatively open.

5.2 Discussion

'He told me... that mine was the middle state, or what might be called the upper state of low life, which he had found by long experience was the best state in the world, the most suited to human happiness' (Daniel Defoe, from *Robinson Crusoe*, 1719). It would be good if teachers in 'middle positions' in school management could take so sanguine a stance. Traditionally the repository for ambitious teachers in the earlier stages of their career, as well as more experienced teachers who do not have either the inclination, ability or encouragement to move beyond their level, middle management has always been a complex and challenging cohort. Three pressures face policy-makers in relation to middle managers in schools.

Firstly there is the need to develop the school leaders of tomorrow. Retention of talented staff in the early stages of their careers has proved to be one of the most enduring problems for this and the previous government. Secondly, though, the subject leadership group has become a focus for development because of their ability to impede or advance wider school improvement. Ofsted reports have identified subject leadership and middle management as key issues for some time. The third pressure relates to primary schools in particular. The national curriculum compromised traditional 'management' because, even in small schools, it has been necessary to devolve authority to subject leaders to a lesser or greater extent. Since the late 1980s, then, there has been a steady move away from the headteacher retaining all the authority and power. In many primary schools, one subject leader may have responsibility for several subjects. It is, therefore, a complex and contradictory situation into which the *Standards for Subject Leaders* have emerged and in which subject leaders carry out their middle management tasks.

The middle manager in a school is always hampered by lack of time. This is a fact. The situation is worsened by the received perception of what constitutes effective subject leadership and the daily reality of management. To a certain extent books like this one only exaggerate the gap between the reality of the complexity and grind of being the manager in the middle and the perception of what the role should be about.

In reality a subject leader is constantly prioritising his or her teaching which takes up almost all of the working day. This means that the management if not the leadership role is pushed to the margins of the day – at lunchtimes and before and after school. Interestingly this is not the case for many senior managers who do have the benefit of a relieved timetable.

As Fullan (1991) points out, an understanding of this 'overload' must be the starting-point for any serious analysis of a teacher's role but this is particularly true of any teacher in a middle management role. The centrality and dominance of the teaching role could be regarded as a good thing, however, if it has an influence on the leadership style adopted by the subject leader. In other words, if the leader is seen as serving the pedagogical aims of the school then it contributes to the learning aims of the school and the subject team.

The complexity of the middle manager's role in the school – indistinguishable as it is from the role of the teacher in the school – is wholly misrepresented by a simplistic, mechanistic model of management which is divorced from an understanding of pupil learning. Field *et al* (2000) have argued convincingly that one of the main contradictions in the subject leader's role is that it is inherently problematic because it involves accountability without responsibility. The middle manager label is particularly inappropriate in the case of primary schools where subject leadership posts are often unremunerated and teachers in them are required to 'manage' senior colleagues without appropriate power and support structures. Management at any level is about interruptions and half-finished tasks. This is particularly true of subject leaders in schools.

When considering the role of the subject leader we need to think first about what we mean by the terms 'subject leadership' and 'middle management'. Gunter (2001) writes about the fact that the so-called 'layer' of middle management is not monolithic and it can be 'contoured' differently according to what tasks are involved with a particular middle manager's job description and where the boundary lies between them and senior management (p106). It is true that the roles clustered under the term 'middle management' are very diverse but there are some common challenges that link all middle managers. Blandford (1997, p4) describes the middle manager's role as 'hybrid' and the sheer complexity of the role is its most striking characteristic.

Although the words 'leadership' and 'management' are used somewhat interchangeably throughout the document, this section is concerned with the activities that have traditionally been associated with management. Blandford (1997, p16) provides an apposite example of the difference between the two concepts: 'At an interview for the post of deputy headteacher in a large (over 1000 pupils), rural, comprehensive I was asked, "What is the difference between a manager and a leader?" My response: *If the task of the team was to climb a mountain, a leader would climb to the top, throw a rope down and ask the team to join him/her. In contrast, a manager would consult his/her team at every stage of the climb which they would then complete together.'*

This is an excellent starting-point from which to consider the role of the manager/leader. It does, of course, present a far more simplistic version of each role than exists in reality because it assumes that the leader has the opportunity to be advancing at a different rate than the others and it assumes a certain leadership style. Fleming (2000) defines good middle managers as 'not trapped in rigid straitjackets but… flexible and adaptable, always on the lookout for ways to improve the education provided by their team. They are able to move easily between roles – teacher, team leader, team member – as required' (p6). We should pause here to consider, though, whether or not this is a good thing.

One of the distinguishing factors of middle management and leadership roles in schools is that usually the subject leader is still engaged in exactly the same tasks and is responding to many of the same pressures as the members of the team. There are few opportunities for subject leaders to engage in leadership activities which are discrete from their other tasks. All you can realistically do is to demonstrate leadership qualities while carrying out the day-to-day activities of the teacher. In some cases the two will coincide. For example, if you are the subject leader for art in a secondary school you will have the opportunity to lead by example and by setting high standards in the leadership of the GCSE coursework moderation and ensuring that your assessment policy reflects this. By way of contrast, though, if you are the subject leader for art in a primary school you may find that the desire to lead other members of the team towards creating an innovative policy on gallery and museum visits in the summer term is seriously compromised by your role as Year 6 class teacher who is taken up with the preparation of students for the key stage 2 Sats. It is therefore important that we exercise a degree of caution when using generic and abstract notions of leadership and management with reference to the subject leader operating in a management structure in a school.

The problem with importing industrial models and ideas about management is that such models fail to take account of the fact that nearly all managers in schools (except, perhaps, heads of very large secondary schools) are still teachers. To put it indelicately, in 'industrial' terms, the managers are still on the shop floor, carrying out the same tasks as those they are leading and monitoring.

Despite the important reforms since 1998 that have restructured the career paths of teachers (the introduction of advanced skills teachers, fast-track teachers, the *Standards* and performance management) it is still the case that, by and large, the most usual route for advancement for teachers is through the steps of management. It was always assumed that good teachers would make good managers and this assumption of ubiquitous competence still prevails. Gunter (2001), though, has pointed out that the introduction of site-based performance management has changed the role of middle management because it is much less child-centred and more accountable to external policy-makers (p108).

A particular challenge facing you is the bridging and intermediate role between junior and senior members of staff and this is what the next section is about. Sometimes this may involve conflict.

5.3 Operational

Fleming and Amesbury (2001) argue that 'The greatest barrier facing the development of an effective middle management layer in the primary school is associated with the history and tradition of this phase of education' (p7). The first thing that you need to bear in mind if you are a subject leader in a primary school, then, is the contradiction that may arise from the culture versus the structure of the school.

One way that this opposition may manifest itself is through the relentless issue of lack of time. As Fleming and Amesbury go on to say, 'middle managers need time to do their job and it is not reasonable to assume that this can all be done after a busy day in the classroom. It is doubtful that many individuals, whether in industry or education, make their best decisions at the end of a difficult or demanding day' (p8). So before we go any further we need to think through the implications of what the effect of operational advice might be on subject leaders who already may be struggling to keep their heads above water. As far as the biggest problem – the lack of time – is concerned, the ideal advice is to try to negotiate for more time. There are several ways of doing this.

■ You could try asking the head and governors for more non-contact time.
■ You could make more use of classroom assistants and other support.

Make a list of professional and non-professional tasks and use the Steven Covey's important versus urgent matrix overleaf (Field *et al*, 2001) to categorise them and then relegate those tasks lacking importance.

If no time is available to create and implement policies in the teaching day, all team work will have to take place after 3.30pm. Although this can work well for subject teams writing policies, it does present something of a conundrum for monitoring the policies. But there are safeguards you can employ to protect your sanity when available time is tight:

1) The feeling that tasks are never complete is damaging and demoralising. You should give yourself just enough things to do that are achievable.

2) Try to negotiate a routine with a colleague where you can have a quiet time at non-contact times during the day. For subject leaders in primary schools an option might be to negotiate a similar routine in the time between the end of school and, say 5.00pm for one or two nights a week.

3) Establish when you work most effectively. For some people this will be the evening while others are at their sharpest first thing in the morning. Once you have decided, you can start to structure your day around your own body clock and allow yourself that time to complete individual tasks.

Task 16	Important versus urgent matrix

Urgent but not important	Important and urgent
Not important and not urgent	**Important but not urgent**

We have established, therefore, that the subject leader is in a rather invidious position regarding the complexity and ambiguities of his or her role. There are also strong cultural forces that conspire against teachers making the most of their time and their talents. An example of this would be if a newly qualified teacher working in a maths department joined the teaching profession in her mid-30s, having taken a few years out after a first career as a management consultant to start a family. She may be a competent but not brilliant classroom teacher but would have much to offer in terms of management of the school (including personnel issues, deployment of resources and time). In the current situation it would be very difficult for such a teacher to progress to a senior management position where she could have the most impact on school-wide management issues without going through the various middle management (including subject leadership) stages first. It could be argued that the headteacher who does not recognise and use her management experience would be unwise and that he or she ought to find a role for such members of staff without necessarily promoting them or making more established teachers feel undermined.

Task 17	The value of non-teaching management experience

INDIVIDUAL TASK

Consider the following questions:

1) Should there be ways of using management experience that has been gained outside teaching in schools?

2) If staff are to be deployed in this way should such a role always carry with it promotional status and remuneration?

Make a list of all the members of your team and by each name write down each person's professional strengths. These can include pedagogical strengths such as being an inspiring teacher or being able to carry out thorough and detailed summative assessments, or they could be more general, professional strengths such as having very high-level 'people skills' and being able to bring cohesion and humour to the most fractious situations. Now ask yourself if you are making the best use of these talents. Are you wasting talent because you are too caught up with the hierarchy of the team? It makes no sense to give the rather brusque and fastidious teacher the responsibility for coordinating the prospective parents' evening just because she is the most experienced member of the team. Far better to use her talents with assessment in the coordination of predicted grades. In the same way, the NQT who is taking a while to gain confidence in the classroom may have a real talent for display and an engaging manner so why not ask him to coordinate the prospective parents' evening? With support he may be able to carry out this task impressively and it will add to his professional self-esteem.

There is another argument that often emerges from the profession, which says that in order to really understand the issues involved in the leadership of teaching and learning activities one must first have a good understanding and considerable experience of the teacher's role. If we regard the role of the subject leader in a restrictive, skills-focused way, the task is basically to manage the various team members in a way that preserves their self-esteem and that allows each of them to make the most valuable contribution to their team, according to their talents. If, however, we regard the issue more deeply, as a leadership dilemma, it is helpful to think about it in terms of the contested values of the team. If you have agreed that a core value of the team's work is to promote staff learning as seriously and as enthusiastically as pupil learning, it is clearly beneficial for the whole team to learn from the most knowledgeable member of staff. It is helpful to consider the dilemma in these terms in order to think strategically.

Gunter (2001, p117) writes about what she describes as the rather normative way that middle management can be written about in the literature: 'It is a pity that a range of voices is often not only silent, but also sometimes ridiculed as claims by subject leaders to be busy is often shown in a negative light rather than the fact that they may be overworked.' It is certainly not my intention in this section to do this; rather, to bear in mind the difficulties while at the same time giving some advice for practical ways forward.

Policies are helpful in relation to the complex issues because they can fulfil a variety of roles, including:

■ helping to demarcate roles
■ offering a sense of fairness
■ articulating the shared values
■ bringing together the team on a shared activity
■ giving change a direction
■ identifying the scope to disagree within a team
■ establishing clear channels of communication between SMT, subject leaders and regular teachers.

In short, policies can go a very long way towards helping to set out clearly the complexities facing the middle manager, and even solving them to a certain extent.

5.4 The management spectrum
Being managed

There is as much to learn about being managed successfully as there is to learn about managing other people and Williams (1995) explores the idea of 'followership' in his work. This is an often ignored fact and it is something that is often overlooked in the sphere of professional development. It is assumed that learning to be a subordinate is something that new professionals will pick up as a matter of course. It is not as simple as that, though. Some might argue that the personal skills involved in being in a middle management position are more demanding than those required of senior managers. This is because typically professionals at this point in their careers have a developed vision about their area of responsibility. No matter how good the senior manager is, the middle manager needs to learn to curb his or her instincts and ideas and to be sensitive to the subtle messages about boundaries and hierarchies that other more senior managers may be giving out. So, when writing policies, try to keep your senior management team involved and try to strike a balance between leading your team and representing its views and understanding your role in relation to whole-school policies and priorities.

Headteachers: The role of the head is crucial. As West (1998, p20) points out, 'middle managers may be able to play a significant role in changing the organisational culture of their schools but much will depend on the headteacher'.

Headteachers can vary greatly in their attitudes and styles of management. Schools also may adopt a leadership panel and subject leaders may find that in fact they have more contact with a deputy or assistant head rather than the headteacher. Whatever the structure of management, though, the head's ideas will hold a great deal of sway over the life and practices of the school. There are a range of leadership styles that tend to be adopted by heads.

Governors: Governors tend to be rather shadowy figures in the lives of teachers, especially in secondary schools. It is sometimes rather difficult to appreciate why people who have no apparent input into the life of the daily running of the school have so much sway over policies and practices. They are, it must be remembered, prime stakeholders in the school and they carry legal responsibility for some aspects of the school curriculum, such as sex and relationships education.

One of the responsibilities of the governors is to help establish (with the head) the aims and policies of the school and to draw up the school development plan. They have an input into how to spend the school budget and into the action plan after an Ofsted inspection. In the last 15 years there have been important changes to the structure and responsibilities of the governing body. This has meant that their power has been increased dramatically. The most important of their increased powers has been the management of the school's budget. So in terms of monetary allocation the subject leader may be directly affected by decisions taken by the governing body and the headteacher. Teachers are also, to a certain extent, accountable to the governors. As the performance tables and value added statistics clearly show how pupils are achieving in each subject, the governors have access to data that may tell them things about the performance of each subject leader's curriculum area.

A guide to communicating with the other stakeholders is to make as many decisions about policy creation and implementation as transparent as possible, while at the same time avoiding bombarding heads and governors with subject-specific information that they do not need to know.

Managing others

One of your challenges is how to keep the values that you espouse as a manager consistent with the values that they demonstrate as teachers. Field (2002, p472) argues that 'The role of the subject leader involves leading and managing. If leadership is concerned with strategy, visions and direction, then the creation of a knowledge base to earn the respect of colleagues and to provide a rationale for decision making is essential'.

Assuming that the subject leader is operating in a happy, effective school culture, the business of managing others should be a fairly simple task of building up a range of skills and styles. This is an assumption, though, that is made far too readily, and too often. School cultures involve powerful forces and particular social and psycho-dynamics will have a significant impact on the way you operate. The *Standards* are clear about the range of tasks that should be developed and mastered by subject leaders (p11). These include helping the staff to sustain enthusiasm as well as their own; appraising staff and auditing their training needs; providing professional development opportunities for members of the team; working with specialist professionals such as Sencos and enabling staff to teach to their best potential.

As anyone who has spent any time in a hierarchical situation knows, however, management is never that simple. The situation is made more complex by staff in schools who are arranged in conflicting and complex situations. A head of history, for example, who may have only been teaching for a couple of years, may find himself or herself in a position of trying to manage the only two other teachers in the department who happen to be the head and the deputy head. Some of these contradictions are dealt with below. One of the core activities for any leader is team-building. Hughes (2004), Field (2004) and Kirkham (2004) all deal with this issue in more detail but it is worth pausing here to consider what we mean by team-building.

The *Standards* put emphasis on this aspect of subject leadership: 'Effective subject leadership results in... teachers who work well together in a team' (p5). There is a recognition not only that teamwork leads to a harmonious working environment in which good staff are retained, but also that it links directly to the overall effectiveness of the central activities of the team. Ofsted research has shown that 'The most effective departments find time for teachers to observe each other's lessons and use this well for different evaluative purposes' (Ofsted – *Good Teaching, Effective Departments*, p59).

This kind of peer observation and evaluation can only really happen in a mutually supportive environment. Where teachers feel threatened or there is unhealthy competition between colleagues this sort of exercise will be unproductive.

Task 18	Audit of the *Standards*

INDIVIDUAL TASK

Look back at the *Standards* listed in the statutory section at the beginning of this chapter. Now audit your own strengths and weaknesses against each standard. This will provide you with an indication of how you need to develop your leadership and management skills.

Motivation is a key element of team-building. There are many schools of thought about what leads to positive motivation. It is important to understand that motivation is actually quite personal and that although the subject leader may be able to encourage the development of an environment in which people feel motivated, they can not take personal responsibility for whether somebody is motivated as a result. Motivation cannot be observed; it is merely the effects of motivation (and for that matter demotivation) – the responses and the changes in behaviour – that can be observed.

Here are some examples of how you can motivate other teachers and celebrate their success:

Teachers in senior positions (for example advanced skills teachers): Although the disadvantages of having senior members of staff teaching in one's subject team are obvious (the blurred line management structure, the prominence of their own commitments and agenda that may conflict with the subject leader's and the trepidation that a subject leader may feel about correcting and steering them) there are also some benefits to the situation. They may be able to assist in monitoring and evaluation activities, for example, once the policies have been written, although this needs to be handled effectively by the subject leaders in order to preserve the trust and goodwill of other members of the subject team.

Teachers in junior positions: The *Standards* and management books often erroneously assume that staff in junior positions are the only ones who are managed by the subject leader. Although this is not the case, they are the ones who are most obviously in this position. Management of this group is likely to be a more simple but no less taxing task than management of one's senior colleagues. Standard 5cvii is concerned with monitoring, supporting, training and assessing NQTs in relation to the NQT standards and with due reference to the Career Entry and Development Profile (CEDP). Use the team tasks throughout this book to ensure that NQTs feel genuinely involved in policy implementation.

Performance management: The DfEE (guidance note 051 *Guidance on Performance Management* 2000) defines 'performance management' thus: 'Throughout the range of documents in the term "appraisal" is synonymous with "performance management". Performance management is the term used to describe the annual professional review and the way this informs pay decisions. Performance review involves professional dialogue about aims and achievements between teachers and their team leaders and headteachers and their governing body. The term "appraisal" is used in the context of the Regulations and primary legislation (the Education No 2 Act 1986).'

It is likely that you will find yourself in the position of 'team leader' – ie, appraiser. You will carry out a performance review of each teacher's work. This works best when it becomes an integral part of the school culture. Performance management and a general continued focus on accountability which has developed rather than diminished under New Labour since 1997, has also, of course, played a part in teachers' motivation to take part in CPD at all levels. Performance management is ongoing and not just an annual 'one-off' event like most models of appraisals and this means that a sustained interest in and a responsibility for one's own professional development is increasingly part of a teacher's perception of his or her own career trajectory.

Other adults: An important and developing area of the work of the subject leader concerns working with other adults and 'non-professional' teachers. The rather misleading term refers to qualified Learning Support Assistants (LSAs) who are taking on an increasing range of the teacher's tasks. The government is keen on developing the role of LSAs, ostensibly to give more time to teachers to complete non-teaching professional tasks in non-contact time. At the time of writing one major teaching union is still registering its opposition to this increased role.

The challenge of working with other adults in the classroom has long been addressed by staff in primary schools and, as they have argued, one of the major challenges is the huge range of expertise and ability that is presented by classroom helpers and classroom assistants. Science technicians also come into this category. You may also have to deal with a range of adults in specialist positions with whom you link, such as field centre managers and peripatetic music teachers, depending on your subject area. Treat all these interested parties as stakeholders and make sure that they all have access to policies that affect their work with you.

Teachers completing initial professional qualifications: You are also likely to have a leadership role in relation to teachers completing initial professional qualifications in your school. There are now a range of routes into teaching, including the traditional higher institution-based PGCE or BA (QTS) qualifications as well as the work-based route such as the graduate teacher scheme. Even if you are not the official mentor you should expect to be observed by new teachers and to engage them in professional conversations.

Bridging the gap

Whatever your particular circumstances, it is still the case that the subject leader must find a way of taking account of the wishes and ideas of those in senior positions while still retaining professional integrity and protecting the integrity and working practices of the members of his or her team. The hierarchical systems in schools are the legacy of over 50 years of development. Although these structures are arguably more transparent and deliberate than ever before, they are still somewhat complex.

Since the late 1980s schools have become increasingly more 'managerial'. As with the example of the head of history outlined earlier, though, even in schools where roles are properly designated and where subject leaders are given appropriate boundaries and areas of responsibility, this can be undermined by the conflict between real power and apparent power. Stephen Ball (1994) has written about the ways in which power is distributed in schools in surreptitious and opaque ways so that people with apparently little official power (a standard scale teacher) may wield inordinate real power – by a close friendship with the headteacher, for example.

5.5 Summary

- Middle management is a hugely complex term which is neither homogenous nor monolithic.
- Some enduring challenges face all middle managers – the lack of time is the most obvious.
- Although middle manager models from industry can be useful, their application to schools is problematic and subject leaders should not feel bad about not living up to these models.
- Subject leaders should think carefully about the link between their values as a teacher and as a subject leader and make sure that all members of the team contribute to policy creation and implementation.

How to write a policy

Objectives

By the end of this chapter you will have:

- understood how to write a good policy

- deconstructed an example of an assessment policy

- considered the use of writing style and understanding of audience when working on policies

- understood ways of developing the team by way of the policy-writing process.

6.1 Regulatory

Section 2 (p5) of the *Standards for Subject Leaders* (TTA, 1998) states that 'Effective subject leadership results in... teachers who work well together as a team; support the aims of the subject and understand how to relate to the school's aims; are involved in the formation of policies and plans and apply them consistently in the classroom'. In other words, it is clear that policy construction and writing should be a shared activity that continues to have an impact on practice from the moment it is first discussed until well after it is written up. As we have established, you will also need to take responsibility for the strategic direction and development of the subject and this will invariably involve the policy-writing process.

The *Standards* also state that subject leaders should be able to 'work as part of a team' and 'acknowledge and utilise the experience, expertise and contribution of others' (p7), so it is very clear that policy is never a solitary pursuit. Among the key skills required of subject leaders are the ability to 'communicate effectively orally and in writing' and to 'negotiate and consult effectively'. Both of these skills are fundamental to the policy-writing process and we shall explore both in this chapter. In addition to these skills and attributes stipulated in the *Standards*, Ofsted will expect subject leaders to have policies on various topics and most subject leaders will have policy formulation and writing as a key responsibility in their job description.

6.2 Discussion

Research shows that effective departments have a clear vision and shared set of values (Harris *et al*, 1995). Policy-writing is a good way to articulate these values and to make them influence all other processes. West (1998, p25) argues that 'All schools have policies, of course, even if it is a policy not to have written policies, which is another way of saying that some schools have relied on implicit policy made up of shared assumptions and tacit understandings, underpinned by custom and norms of

Subject leadership: policy implementation   55

practice. Such a stance may work effectively during times of stability but becomes highly problematic in times of turbulence and change.'

Task 19	Effective school policies

INDIVIDUAL TASK

Find an example of a school policy that is effective and one that you feel more cynical about. Don't share this with the team – you don't want to 'stir up' subversion! Now, using different-coloured pens, underline parts of the good one that contribute to its success and parts of the weaker policy that make it less convincing.

Of course, as we have established in previous chapters, teachers have been working through a period of rapid and profound change for the past 15 years and therefore an absence of written policies is no longer an option – not least because in many schools the turnover of staff is so high that attempting to operate without written policies is like building a house without solid foundations. So policies might provide a sense of stability and security for harassed teachers.

Task 20	Collecting useful school policies

TEAM TASK

Use the area below to make a list of the school policies that you actually use in your work. Be honest.

- ■
- ■
- ■
- ■

Now think of three characteristics that the policies have in common and that mark these policies out from the ones that are less well used.

- ■
- ■
- ■

School effectiveness research (MacGilchrist *et al*, 1995) shows that there is a clear link between shared planning and improving schools. The sharing of professional dialogue is as important as the planning itself.

Policies can serve practical purposes as well as articulating philosophical positions. In particular, as we have seen in previous chapters, they can further managerial aims. Field *et al* (2000, p161) argue that policies can protect teachers from the impact of macro-political pressures (such as social and political change) by providing a sense of stability and security. This raises questions about teachers' professionalism, though. The job is inherently complex and, at times, exhausting. Should we really, then, promote and comply with the idea that at times of stress the first thing that suffers is teachers' ability to engage in critical debate with macro-policy and, instead, they simply operate on 'auto-pilot', shielded from government demands by bland, internal interpretations of it?

Perhaps there is a middle position. If the professional values articulated in the policy documents are strong enough to lend direction to the activities of the team but also general enough to provide space for teachers to adjust to new developments, they can support genuinely reflective practice rather than hindering it. The 'shielding' nature of internal policies is only viable if they are articulated and shared by the team. In this way, written policies can give voice to a shared vision of the integrity of the subject. Field *et al* (2000, p166) espouse a sanguine view of policies: 'Policy-writing provides support, lifts morale, highlights expertise and contributes to the development of a culture of collegiality and collaboration'.

This brings us to one of the key points associated with effective policy-writing: the process is as important as the product. Policy-writing is a perfect opportunity to reflect on practice. The work of Donald Schön (1983), among others, has caused a great deal of professional development work in education to be predicated on the idea of 'reflective practice'. Reflection is often conceived rather narrowly as a private, introspective activity, and, of course, this is possible. But the Vygotskiian idea of learning in a social setting is sometimes overlooked, as is the inextricable link between reflection and action. The process of talking about, constructing and writing a policy provides the ideal environment for joint professional learning to take place and for planned action to inform real action. In other words, to bridge the gap between theory and practice.

It is often assumed that policies are communicated in a direct, linear fashion, from the governors and senior management team through subject leaders to class teachers and other staff. This, of course, is a simplistic misrepresentation of what actually happens. Networks of communication are inherently complex and prone to breaking down. Communication is never a simple case of sending and receiving messages. Communication is always surrounded by what some linguists call 'noise'. 'Noise' can be taken literally but it can also mean those differences in individuals which confound and complicate the ability of people to understand one another. So you need to understand that whatever is agreed in discussions of how the policy will be formulated, different teachers will necessarily implement the ideas in their own way. Also, because channels of communication between senior management and the staff are likely to break and burst, this will affect the ultimate implication of policy. Allowance needs to be made for this when writing it.

If the policy is agreed on (and, by definition, it should be agreed on and selected as a way of guiding future action), the potential for the team to develop is rich. This can only happen, though, if the number and length of the policy documents is rationalised. As West (1998, p25) argues, 'too many policies produced in too short a time is likely to result in a massive implementation overload and token adoption'. He counsels the need to avoid 'paper fatigue'.

Also policy writing following a backward mapping process (Elmore, 1979) ensures that the 'workers' are involved and have a sense of ownership. It is vitally important not to lose sight of the main purpose of the policy which is to articulate and sometimes to improve on professional practice. Policy-writing should be an empowering activity. Policies articulate where the school as an institution (an employer, a centre of learning, a social centre and a community centre) is going. This is a noble and challenging task and should be treated as such. Policy production should therefore be a learning opportunity for all who take part. A policy produced in isolation is not just an impotent document. It is a lost learning opportunity for the subject leader, the team and the institution.

6.3 Writing, thought and practice

It almost goes without saying that most policies are written down but this is another level of complexity in the process. The act of writing has a very sophisticated relationship with thought and emotion. By writing something down we can appear to make the complex simple and the uncontrollable tamed, but doing so can also distort what we regard as the truth. Some senior and middle managers may be tempted to think that just because they have written a policy down it is a manifestation of practice. Worse, ineffective leaders may try to use the written policy as a substitute for practice – as if by saying that something happens it makes it happen. We need to accept that the policies need to serve an active purpose which goes beyond simply accounting for what is already happening; policies need to be prescriptive as well as descriptive.

Life is chaotic. Every day we encounter numerous unpredictable occurrences that we can only make sense of by converting them to narrative. The story of our day ('I've had a bad day') our week, or our life can all be rendered less threatening and more manageable by framing them in a narrative and thinking about them as stories. Writing, including prosaic non-fiction writing like a report or a policy, helps us to control our version of reality. Even a shopping list helps us to quantify and make reasonable our multiple and infinite needs and wants. For a schoolteacher who is also a subject leader this sense of chaos is particularly acute. There are many pressures on teachers that make their professional experience unique. These pressures include constant questions from colleagues and a huge number of interactions in a day. It is a natural response to want to control this experience, and the process of writing a policy, with its neat prose, is tempting. Middle management in a school is often characterised by a series of interruptions. All management activities are therefore grafted onto the central activity of teaching. We may want to draw all this multifaceted experience together in a written document. However, the desire to impose one's own sense of reality on a team can lead to failure and the fewer people involved in writing the policy, the more likely it is to fail. If the gap between the reality as it is represented in the written document produced by the team leader and reality as it appears to members of the team is too wide, the policy is rendered invalid and the trust and investment of the team are jeopardised.

Any piece of writing should have a defined sense of purpose and audience in order to be effective. The purpose of the policy document should be:

- to make concrete the practice that already happens or should happen
- to enhance quality
- to explain the principles underpinning this practice.

The audience should primarily be the stakeholders – the teachers in the subject team, the senior management team, the governors and, where appropriate, the pupils and the parents. A secondary audience will be internal and external quality assurance bodies such as Ofsted. Policies will inevitably form part of the quality assurance procedure and it should always be borne in mind that policy documents are not merely internal documents, but they should certainly not be written with the external audience primarily in mind. An ill-defined purpose and sense of audience leads to policies which are not respected by any of the stakeholders and that become, instead, mere pieces of paperwork.

6.4 Operational

Before a policy is developed it is important to first find out where the strengths and weaknesses of the subject and subject team are in relation to the policy. It is also necessary to discover where institutional fault lines might lie in relation to the policy as these may have a hindering or liberating effect on the policy implementation. For example, the development of a subject policy for teaching gifted and talented children will run a very different course in a primary school or a grammar school because of the different ideological frameworks within which the teachers are working. Auditing is essential at this stage and there are a number of ways of doing this, such as SWOT (strengths, weaknesses, opportunities and threats) analysis or force field analysis; other writers (Field *et al*, 2000) advocate these methods. It is sometimes more useful, though, to restrict this stage of the policy development to the simplest of terms. Sometimes it is best just to describe the situation, without value-laden judgments at this stage.

So, for example, when constructing an assessment policy if you are a subject leader for maths, you may ask the team to simply note how often each of them writes a positive comment in students' workbooks. The sense of security among teachers at this stage is dependent on the subject leader's ability to build a safe learning environment, as we have previously discussed. So, '15% of comments included a positive, personal message' is all that is required of teachers to take note. These readings are then brought to the whole team and a bigger picture becomes available. It is difficult to get a true picture of the situation if reports of it are 'filtered' through an evaluative eye so you need to make it clear that they, not anyone else, will be making judgments about professionalism at this point.

West (1998, p26) warns subject leaders to 'make sure that the learning within the staff group is at least equal to, or greater than, the changes you are trying to bring about' and part of this is the creation, from the outset, of systems designed to shape the actions upon which firm, agreed principles are based.

This reflective nature of the process of building the policy is vitally important. If you adopt a consultative leadership style, it is important to remember that there may well be as many different ideas about what goes into the policy as there are teachers in the team. You would be wise, then, to strive for representation rather than individualism (Field *et al*, 2001, p169) in the inclusion of views.

A suggested order of activities in terms of creating the policy is given below. It might be worth carrying out a 'paper trail' throughout the process to measure how all of these points relate to the whole-school aims and documentation. So, for each of the stages completed, link back to the whole-school development plan. Two questions that should inform all of the above activities are 'where are you going?' and 'what are we doing?'

When structuring the writing process, subject leaders may want to work in the following way:

Task 21	Sequence of policy-writing activities

1) Agree the purpose and objectives for the policy and include quality assurance mechanisms at this early stage.

2) Brainstorm colleagues' ideas: you could use a visual map around the classroom or create an 'innovation map' in which you and colleagues draw, write and find other ways to visually represent your ideas about the policy and post these ideas around a classroom wall.

3) Clarify the brief with the senior management team and other stakeholders.

4) Discuss, argue about, and finally agree on the subject team's philosophical approach to the subject of the policy.

5) Discuss the contextual advantages of the school and institutional constraints.

6) Begin to translate these ideas onto an agreed proforma.

7) Produce a draft of the policy.

8) Circulate the draft.

9) Consult the senior management team.

10) Redraft after consideration of stakeholders' comments.

11) Evaluate the written policy against the originally agreed aims and objectives.

Policies can be set out in a number of ways and they will include, in some form or other:
■　reference to the school's mission
■　a description of responsibilities relating to the policy
■　how these responsibilities fit into the existing hierarchy
■　monitoring and evaluation procedures
■　the purpose of the policy
■　modes of internal and external channels of communication
■　criteria for inclusion of ideas and review.

| Task 22 | Writing a critique of a draft policy |

TEAM TASK

Examine the draft policy on assessment below. It contains some of the ideas set out above but some are missing. First, ask the team to annotate the policy, pointing out positive and negative elements, working in the same way that you did with Task 19. Remember to look at how well the policy demonstrates the key ideas of purpose, audience and bridging the gap between reality and ideals. Write the comments in the box provided at the end of the policy. Now discuss your ideas as a group. When you have thoroughly deconstructed this policy consider the elements that you intend to adopt when constructing the team's policy proforma (see Task 23) and those you want to discard.

Draft policy on assessment

1. Key principles

  1) All assessment should inform the learning.

  2) A range of assessment methods should be used.

  3) All assessment should be accompanied by effective feedback.

The means by which key principles are addressed is indicated in Section 3 (summary of the assessment procedures).

2. Key characteristics of effective assessment

  1) All grades and levels are accompanied by written comments.

  2) Pupils have plenty of opportunities to discuss assessments with teachers.

  3) Assessments are valid and reliable.

  4) A range of tasks are assessed, including informal, draft tasks and oral tasks as well as formal, finished pieces of work.

  5) Assessments should have clear aims and inform future teaching.

  6) Pupils should have a clear understanding of what they are being assessed on.

  7) Records should be clear, concise and not burdensome.

3. Summary of the assessment procedures in relation to the key principles

- Assessment tasks are planned to enable the pupils to understand their progress according to the national curriculum and to set their own targets. To enable them to do this they have their own copy of the record sheet.

- Similarly the range of assessment tasks allows a flexibility of choice in terms of topics to be covered and to ensure that all pupils have an opportunity to shine according to their learning style preference.

- More detailed information in relation to the individual courses can be found in the individual schemes of work/medium-term plans.

- Baseline and Sats assessment data, as well as Cat scores are made available to all subject teachers and there is an expectation that this data will be used to inform planning and teaching.

- No effort grades will be given for pupils' work.

Task 22 **Writing a critique of a draft policy** *continued*

4. Marking

The reasons for marking are:

- to help pupils to learn more effectively
- to provide parents with information about their child's progress
- to help teachers to gain a full understanding of pupils' strengths and weaknesses and the pace of learning.

There are no guidelines about the colour of pens used by teachers but it is our policy that all written comments should be legible and the comments should be encouraging and positive and be accompanied by a target.

5. Monitoring, evaluation and review

Teachers in the subject team are paired and regularly cross-moderate pupils' work. One team meeting per term is given over to whole-team moderation of pupils' work.

Monitoring of this policy is ongoing. The subject leader regularly examines a sample of assessment across year groups. This data is evaluated by the team termly. The policy will be reviewed in the summer term with the senior management team in relation to the school development plan.

Appendices

- National curriculum levels in relation to this subject
- Syllabus examination criteria for this subject
- Minutes of the meetings that led to the creation of this agreed policy

Comments on the draft policy

1) How clearly are the aims of the policy expressed?
2) How well does the policy address its intended audience?
3) Are the intended outcomes of the policy expressed effectively?
4) How do you think that the key stakeholders will respond to this policy?

6.5 The writing style

When writing the policy, it is a good idea to bear a few things in mind.

1) Use inclusive pronouns ('we' rather than 'I' or 'you'). This will help to make people feel included, and to own the policy and have an input in its implementation and success. It is common sense that the policy will have more chance of being implemented properly if it is adopted by all members of the team rather than appearing to belong to the subject leader and to be imposed on everyone else.

2) Try to avoid using an overbearing or dictatorial tone. Measure where the statements you are using come in the continuum of leadership styles. Make sure that the tone of the language matches other aspects of your leadership style.

3) Try to aim for a balance between professional vocabulary and accessibility. Avoid acronyms as much as possible. Jargon is not only offputting to anybody

outside the core group but can also close down the freedom of both thought and expression. It is important to have professional 'ownership' of the language: by importing government terms wholesale, the policy may appear to be simply a statement of powers outside the school.

4) Use short points rather than writing an essay. This does not mean, however, that you need to avoid research references – the policy will be deepened and enriched by reference to theory and considered reference to national policy. Make points action-oriented and keep the whole statement simple.

Task 23	Policy-writing proforma

TEAM TASK

This is an example of a proforma that you could use for constructing policies:

- Short outline of why the policy is needed (eg school or government directive or a perceived lack in current practice).
- Statement of aims and objectives and criteria for success.
- Two or three guiding principles

1

2

3

- Three principles of policy in the subject area

1

2

3

- Exact guidelines about how this can impact on practice.
- Resourcing issues (including time/staff and books etc).
- Quality assurance procedures (anonymity, evaluation etc).
- Consider the overarching question: how does the policy contribute to furthering the quality of learning?
- Guidelines for staff for implementing it, including real examples.

Attach appendices including arrangements for staffing; timing; relevant national and international data and a glossary of terms.

When you have decided how you want to work, involve the team in the policy construction. Email can be very helpful in the drafting and consulting stages and you can ask stakeholders to highlight their changes in colour. When working through the drafting stages of producing the document it is worth scheduling some time to meet and to talk about process – this should not be incidental.

Always bear in mind West's (1998, p26) advice: 'Wherever possible, don't act until you are conceptually clear about what you are trying to do'. He goes on to say that in the early stages 'Iconoclasm and the capacity to think divergently should be encouraged within the group'. It is your task to combine these ideas and to keep in only the points that will result in long-term benefits for teaching and learning.

6.6 Summary

- The process of creating the policy is as important as the policy itself.
- Subject leaders need to adopt an approach to the leadership style – it is determined by their reading of the situation.
- The structure of the policy should link with the aims of the school.
- The choice of vocabulary and tone should be accessible and professional.

Effective learning

Chapter 7

> **Objectives**
>
> By the end of the chapter you will have:
>
> - explored the meanings of the term 'effective learning'
>
> - understood why effective learning is so important to the development of policies
>
> - appreciated that an understanding of learning should form the basis of other subject leadership activities
>
> - started to articulate your own philosophy of effective learning
>
> - made a plan for the development of an effective learning policy in your subject area.

7.1 Regulatory

There are good professional and academic arguments for making effective learning the foundation on which to base all other policies. As West (1998, p28) argues, 'a policy for teaching and learning lies at the heart of a school and is central to all that happens. The formulation of that generic policy will be the biggest investment a school makes on behalf of the pupils the staff seek to serve'. The academic arguments will be examined further on in this chapter but first we will look at the statutory obligations of the subject leader regarding the development and promotion of an effective learning policy.

The *Standards for Subject Leaders* (TTA, 1998) tell us that the core purpose of the subject leader is 'to provide professional leadership and management for a subject to secure high-quality teaching, effective use of resources and improve standards of learning and achievement for all pupils' (p4).

The connection is made, therefore, between learning and leadership and implicit in the *Standards* is the expectation that, by leading the subject effectively, subject leaders will be able to bring about high levels of learning. Research suggests that learning is not so simple a process. Real learning is, in fact, a complex and often accidental process that is elusive and not particularly malleable to simplistic measuring mechanisms. We shall explore more of this in the section below. On a basic level, though, the subject leader needs to understand the link between learning and achievement and to manage the subject in such a way that teaching is of high quality and produces appropriate intended outcomes.

The *Standards* also state (section A, p10) that subject leaders should 'develop and implement policies and practices for the subject which reflect the school's commitment to high achievement and effective teaching and learning'.

So, you need to be clear about your team's philosophy of teaching and learning and how it fits into the other policies. But first they must develop the effective learning policy itself. The national strategy for CPD (DfEE, 2001) suggests that the way forward for teachers' development is to learn from other teachers' successes and experience.

7.2　Discussion

Task 24　Team learning

TEAM TASK
Ask the team to write down three examples of a situation where you have learned something effectively. Share these ideas as a team. Note down what are the common conditions necessary for effective learning.
Now do the reverse: write down an ineffective learning experience. Think about your life in general, not just the academic and professional aspects of your life. It might be learning how to drive or something more personal like learning how to be managed. Again, talk to other members of your team and use the experiences as a starting point for a discussion about the conditions that are neccessary for effective learning to take place.

Learning always involves change. It could be a change in understanding, a change in perception or a change in practice. At its deepest level the learner changes. Learning is about doing something new and different. Learning is always individual because it happens due to the particular configurations of our brains. The problem with schools is that we often overvalue the aspects of learning that are measurable rather than measuring what is most valuable. There needs to be a complete cycle in which knowledge is not truly learned until it is reflected on and applied to real life. All of this is true not just for the pupils but for ourselves too, and we need to think about how it has an impact on the writing of policies and the policies themselves.

The centrality of learning to all activities is the key feature of all effective and improving schools. Research (MacGilchrist *et al*, 1997) shows that where teachers see themselves as learners and take their learning seriously, this sets up a virtuous cycle in which the students are also encouraged to discuss and celebrate their own learning and to develop a meta-learning vocabulary. There is, though, an inherent contradiction here. The focus on learning for the sake of 'raising standards', as is the case with political interpretations of school improvement research, can, paradoxically, lead to the dilution of factors necessary for the secure learning environment, such as the ability to make mistakes in a blame-free environment and the freedom to explore cognitive cul-de-sacs and blind alleys in the learning process. The intense assessment agenda can jeopardise the secure learning environment that it so fundamental to getting 'good results'.

Two factors distinguish effective departments from the less effective ones. The first is that the subject leader is widely regarded as an expert in his or her subject area and they have a considered, confident subject pedagogy. The second factor is that these departments are characterised by teaching and learning as the main focus of the team's work. So, subject leaders and their teams need to develop an understanding of pedagogy in their subject and to develop their thinking about why their subject is important. Field *et al* (2000) point out that discussions about the integrity of the subject in a cross-curricular context are a crucial foundation on which to develop an effective learning policy in the subject.

A look at Bloom's taxonomy of knowledge shows us that the more difficult and sophisticated types of learning (located at the top of the taxonomy) are often given the least time in classroom and homework activities by teachers in their planning.

Task 25	Bloom's taxonomy

TEAM TASK

Take a look at the taxonomy with your team and annotate it with activities from the past couple of days. Discuss the spread of thinking skills and how you can improve it.

Type of Learning	Activities
■ Evaluation	
■ Synthesis	
■ Application	
■ Understanding	
■ Knowledge	

7.3 Students' learning

There are many theories of how children learn. These include the so-called 'behaviourist' models which concentrate on the individual's reflex responses and the way that humans, in common with other animals, work for rewards. More sophisticated models, concentrating on the environmental factors necessary for learning in humans, are clustered in a broad group known as social constructivist. These theories are based on the idea that humans are basically social animals that operate in packs. Uniquely, human beings have developed a sophisticated language system and some social constructivists regard this as the basis for all learning.

Vygotsky, the Russian psychologist from the early part of the last century, argued not only that language was the main component of learning but also that a learner could continually extend his or her repertoire of competence with the help of a teacher who could enable the learner to scaffold his or her learning in a zone of proximal development. Piaget argued that this supportive learning experience could be facilitated by peers and that, in fact, in the case of children, this was more effective because there was no hierarchy involved as there would be with a teacher/pupil situation. We learn by reflecting on new knowledge and then having an opportunity to apply it. The interdependent organic nature of learning, assessment, teacher characteristics, student characteristics and learning environment means that we cannot talk about students' learning in isolation from other factors. The model can be applied equally to the school classroom or to an adult professional in a learning situation.

7.4 Adult learning

It is a good idea if teachers are also learners. As Seneca the Younger said, 'Even while they teach they learn' – thus highlighting the inextricability of teaching and learning. Although the two processes are not interchangeable (there are plenty of teachers who do not learn) they feed off each other productively.

Teachers tend to know a good deal about children's learning but less about adults' learning. For the subject leader, knowledge about how and why adults learn is as important as an understanding of pedagogy. In the previous section we examined how departmental cultures that support learning are characteristic of effective departments. It is wise to remember that staff learning is as important as the pupils' learning and in fact it should come from the same impetus. The study of adult learning, known as andragogy, focuses on the part played by the learner's self-concept and the importance of the learner's previous experience in the learning process.

Many subject leaders will already be well aware of the power of the varying levels of experience of many members of the team. Subject leaders often feel the benefit of having older and wiser members in their subject group. It has to be said, though, that levels of experience can also have a negative effect if used to challenge the subject leader without genuine reason. By making the department a learning department the subject leader can use the skills and experience of the members of the team to the benefit of the rest of the team while making a potentially disaffected person feel valued.

For example, a young male subject leader of PE in a primary school inherits a core team of teachers which includes an NQT, a part-time teacher and a very experienced teacher in her mid-50s. These teachers have opted to be part of the PE planning group because they feel a particular affinity towards the subject. From the outset the subject leader has noticed a definite antipathy towards him and his ideas coming from the older teacher. She attends all meetings but refuses to make eye contact when he is speaking to the group and she neatly sabotages his plans for improvement of the subject and the new proforma that he introduces in order to standardise medium-term planning. After a few weeks of adopting the inclusive, democratic leadership style without much success, the subject leader decides to take another tack. He rethinks the way that he is using subject team meetings and arranges them so that administrative work takes up only 10 minutes at the end of the meeting and he uses email and paperwork in between meetings to keep everybody up to date. The bulk of the meeting, he announces, is now to be used for professional learning. This will take a number of guises. Some team meetings will take the form of seminars and others will be led by members of the team in their areas of strength. He has noticed that although the most experienced teacher tends to adopt a fairly narrow range of styles, her behaviour management is excellent – far better than anybody else's in the team and the NQT in particular could greatly benefit from help in this area. So the subject leader decides on a similar area of strength for each member of the team and arranges a timetable of seminars in the scheduled meeting slots when each member can lead a seminar. In this way the previously disaffected member of the team is able to articulate strengths in her own practice, which is a learning experience in itself, and the others benefit from observing her.

Another way of using departmental meeting time to enhance the professional learning of the team is to ask the team to read a piece of published research before the meeting and then use part of the allocated meeting time to scrutinise and discuss it in the context of the school's and team's work. Below are some ideas for how to make subject team meetings more learning-focused.

Task 26	Making meetings meaningful

Experiment with the following activities in your leadership of team meetings.

Activity	Benefits
Rotate the chair of the meeting.	Each member of the team learns to lead in a supportive environment and you are freed to take a more participatory role in discussions.
Routinely ask team members to read a piece of research related to one of the topics for discussion.	By starting the meeting with a seminar-style response to the research you allow the team to stand back from the details of implementation. Theory can inform practice and provide new perspectives on the team's activities.
Team members conduct small-scale action research projects.	Areas identified on the action plan can be focused on and recommendations made for improvements.

Task 26	Making meetings meaningful *continued*

Activity	Benefits
A regular portion of the meeting is given over to discussing the team's independent learning activities.	This encourages the team to undertake professional and non-professional learning activities. Links can be made between reading, research and practice. Team members feel that their learning is recognised and relevant.
Mentor student teachers and ask them to bring in theoretical perspectives on the team's practice.	Mentoring has been linked to school improvement (Field and Philpott, 1999) and where there are pairs or more of student teachers in a department these benefits may be even more significant (Sorensen *et al*, 2002).

7.5　Professional learning

If you are serious about developing the learning department then you need to put as much thought into developing the policy for effective learning among members of the subject team as you do into developing the policy for effective student learning. Schön (1983) has written a good deal about the need for professionals to be reflective as they learn and develop, and Gunter (2001) has written about the need to develop dissent in professional dialogue.

Not all professional learning happens in a conventional, academic way, though. Peer- and line-managed mentoring and shadowing are rich forms of learning for all involved. We should also not neglect the humble conversation as a form of professional learning, often overlooked as a soundtrack to the 'real' business of teaching and learning or assessment. It is in conversation that sometimes we make the most startling discoveries about how to improve our practice and also where we articulate for the first time some of our emerging ideas about what we do.

The national strategy for CPD presents professional learning as being at the core of school improvement. The idea that external forces (such as poverty, post-industrial changes to what we regard as the workplace and the old-fashioned ideas of the varying stages of psychological development) might have a greater influence on pupil success or otherwise at school then the professionalism of the teacher or headteacher is nowhere to be seen in the document. This is not surprising and it is consistent with the ideological assumptions that underpin the *Standards*.

The DfEE defines CPD as being '...all about making sure that teachers have the finest and most up-to-date tools to do their job' and it links this definition to 'a renewed sense of teaching as a profession' (DfEE, 2000).

This demonstrates a somewhat narrow, utilitarian view of professional development manifested in the craft-based analogy 'tools' referred to in the *Standards* – a word linked to mechanical, practical activities. There is an interesting nuance set up by the words 'profession' and 'tool'. It could be argued that a mature profession is able to define its own competences – and the setting-up of the GTC has gone some way towards this – but the fact remains that, however useful the *Standards* prove to be, they have still been imposed on the profession by the government.

7.6 Use of research

If you are going to use research in seminar sections of team meetings, team members must have access to the most appropriate material. The most current research which is subject-based will be most likely to be disseminated by the subject associations. It is possible for a department or whole school to become a member of most associations and, indeed, you could make this a central part of your teaching and learning policy. Do not forget that there is a good deal of research into generic educational matters also available. These include assessment, learning, inclusion issues and cross-curricular issues such as citizenship. These are also available in journals and books as well as from the associations such as British Education Research Association (BERA) and the International Professional Development Association (IPDA). National educational publications (such as *The Times Educational Supplement*) help to bring issues to public notice.

You may be enrolled in CPD activities that are situated in educational institutions such as universities. An example might be a postgraduate diploma in subject leadership such as the one run by Canterbury Christ Church University College. Other members of the subject team may also be engaged in similar activities.

Whether as part of the written requirement for such a course or due to the demands of a government or LEA study award, you may find that a team member needs to complete some action research. This is a research paradigm that is closely allied to the idea of the reflective practitioner. In this model of research the teacher identifies an issue or a problem and then gathers data from his or her professional situation and sets out a plan to effect some sort of change process. The issue or paradigm is then revisited to complete the cycle and potentially to begin a further cycle of action research. It is a useful paradigm because the research serves the practice directly.

We must not forget that much learning takes place accidentally. This is what is sometimes referred to as 'learning on the job' but sometimes it happens in a completely unrelated situation. Again, we must bear this in mind when creating policies because it means that the learning will happen in all sorts of incidental ways as the team works through the stages of policy-writing identified in the previous chapter.

7.7 Effective learning and effective teaching

Ideally learning should be at the centre of the team's activities. A common understanding of the characteristics of effective learning should certainly underpin teaching. Within the context of discussions about how to promote effective learning the subject leader should be able to influence members of the team to adopt a wider repertoire of teaching styles. A policy on teaching and learning could include advice on how to do this.

A way of influencing this as a subject leader is to make the paperwork support the learning process rather than simply running alongside it. On medium-term plans, you could encourage teachers to identify the type of teaching style adopted in each section of a lesson – for a sample of lessons each week, for example.

In the next chapter we will examine how, once these processes have been started, the subject leader is able to measure and monitor their success.

7.8 Operational

It is important to get the policy on learning and teaching right because if it works it can underpin all the other policies, thus avoiding the need for repetition and rewriting and distraction from the main teaching and learning focus of the subject department. Below are the characteristics of an effective subject team that takes its own learning as seriously as the pupils' learning.

Some schools have teaching and learning as a permanent feature on departmental agendas. A teacher must describe an activity which has worked well. In every heads of department (HoDs) meeting, HoDs must report on an activity from the department meeting that worked well. In every SMT meeting the deputy (curriculum) reports on a teaching and learning activity that worked well, emanating from the HoDs meeting. Teaching and learning is therefore the focus of every meeting.

Characteristics of the learning subject team

1) Department meetings include a seminar-style input in which political and theoretical perspectives are discussed in the light of current practice.
2) Teachers often talk about learning.
3) Teachers are all involved in their own learning, whether it be studying for diplomas or masters' degrees in education or attending adult education classes on yoga or interior design. The learning process itself is more important than the content of what is learned. Teachers need to be in touch with what it feels like to be a learner and all the feelings of exhilaration and failure that are involved in learning.
4) Students are spoken about in terms of their learning capacity or potential rather than their ability or behaviour. This should go beyond superficial political correctness and be about a genuine engagement with thinking and talking about learning.
5) Everyone in the teaching team has a good idea of how they learn most effectively.

> **Task 27**   **Characteristics of the learning subject team**
>
> Look at the characteristics of the learning subject team (above) and consider the extent to which you and your team demonstrate these characteristics.

When creating the learning policy, subject leaders should first answer the following questions with their team:

1) What is the team's shared understanding of effective learning and which learning theories have informed this view?
2) What is particular about the way your subject approaches teaching and learning and what does it have in common with other subjects?
3) What professional repertoire are teachers expected to have who teach in this subject and how can the team help to increase the repertoire of its members?

If the teaching and learning policy is strong, all the schemes of work can come out of it. It is important that subject leaders and their teams first develop their own understanding of what constitutes effective learning before they interpret it into policies and plans to support that view. It is also important that they link their view of effective learning to an understanding of what happens in terms of improved practice.

Assessment should not be regarded as the end product of the learning process, but as part of it in an organic way. The quality and appropriateness of the assessment methods used will have an impact on the way that teachers and students feel about the learning process.

7.9 Summary

- The policy on effective learning should be central to all the other policies and all subject team activities.
- Meetings should become opportunities for team members to learn from each other and to examine relevant research.
- Learning should be the focus of the team's work and all other activities should support the goal of increasing the effectiveness of pupil learning.
- You should encourage the team to develop their own learning activities. This could take the form of focused professional development or it could be quality learning about unrelated ideas. Because of the nature of teaching, simply experiencing what it feels like to be a learner will always improve teaching practice if it is reflected on.
- You should actively create opportunities for individual and group reflection. These could be linked to research, shadowing and mentoring activities or professional conversations.
- The learning and teaching policy should include provision for staff learning, or a separate policy on staff learning within the team should be created.

Monitoring, evaluation and review of policies

Chapter 8

> **Objectives**
>
> By the end of this chapter you will have:
>
> ■ examined a variety of methods of monitoring, evaluating and reviewing learning according to policy areas
>
> ■ explored the distinctions between monitoring and evaluation and review
>
> ■ understood the need for clear success criteria and a shared philosophy with the team.

8.1 Regulatory

If policies are to be successful then their effectiveness needs to be monitored. This chapter explores the monitoring, evaluation and review processes in order to provide subject teachers with some useful professional tools for the quality aspect of policy implementation. Monitoring, evaluation and review are three stages in a process which, taken at a simple level, represent quality assurance procedures through which subject leaders can assess the effectiveness of their policies through teaching and learning. The *Standards for Subject Leaders* (TTA, 1998) make it clear that there is a distinct area of responsibility regarding monitoring, evaluation and review. We are told that 'Subject leaders evaluate the effectiveness of teaching and learning, the subject curriculum and progress towards targets for pupils and staff, to inform future priorities and targets for the subject. The degree to which a subject leader is involved in monitoring to provide a range of information for evaluation will depend on school policy and be influenced by the size of the school. Although the subject leader will undertake a variety of monitoring activities, headteachers in smaller primary schools may retain a larger proportion of that monitoring which requires direct classroom observation of teaching and learning' (p4).

So, depending on the size of the school and its specific context, you will have a minor or major input into whole-school and subject monitoring, evaluation and review strategies of generic policies. This increases to a great deal of input when the area of responsibility relates to the monitoring, evaluation and review of subject-specific policies.

The *Standards* also state that the effectiveness of the subject leader will depend on '...the assessment procedures and systems for monitoring and recording progress – for example, how subject leaders contribute to the school assessment, recording and reporting arrangements' (p9). On a statutory level, then, you are required to take responsibility for quality assurance in your subject area. As we will go on to discover in this chapter, though, there are far more convincing reasons linked to effective practice that make monitoring, evaluation and review important and interesting pursuits for the subject leader.

There is also emphasis in the *Standards* on the need to collect data, in order to gain an understanding of pupils' progress and, by implication, of the effectiveness of those policies leading to teaching and learning. You will be expected to evaluate the effectiveness of teaching directly and (Avii), therefore, 'monitor the progress made in achieving subject plans and targets, evaluate the effects on teaching and learning, and use this analysis to guide further improvement' (p10).

The emphasis on establishing systems that can provide data on progress or otherwise runs throughout the *Standards* and is echoed in other areas of DfES documentation. There is also need for monitoring for the threshold standards which is incumbent on subject leaders to complete. Ofsted inspectors will also expect subject leaders to have evidence gathered from monitoring their subjects (Bell and Ritchie, 1999, p39). The key stage 3 national strategy states that the core roles for subject leaders are:

1)   making judgments about pupils' performance
2)   evaluating teaching and learning and setting priorities for improvement
3)   leading sustainable improvement by identifying targets for improvement (p2).

Subject leaders, it states, should make judgments about pupils' attainment and 'systematically observe colleagues teaching and have the skills needed to feed back constructively and objectively... They monitor the planning of teaching in their subject' (p3 Field *et al,* 2001). According to the document, subject leaders are responsible for supporting school policy on monitoring and evaluating teaching quality. Specifically, they are required to observe teaching and feed back to colleagues, and to review teachers' planning. They should also monitor the impact of teaching across groups of pupils (p5). The findings from this monitoring process should be used, along with analysis of pupil attainment data, in regular reviews of work towards the targets. The strategy gives ideas of how to set up such monitoring systems and it suggests that effective ways of teaching different aspects of the subject should be discussed at departmental meetings.

Other reasons why monitoring is a fundamental part of the subject leader's work are that:

1)   it is an essential stage in the planning process
2)   it contributes to the process of team leadership because the findings can be used to plan not just teaching activities but also staff learning activities
3)   the findings can be used as a basis for reflection with the team about how established principles about the subject are being implemented
4)   it should acknowledge success
5)   it prepares the team for Ofsted and internal scrutiny procedures
6)   it is a useful way of monitoring student progress.

Overall it is worth remembering that in a school where learning is at the centre of everything it is imperative that learning is promoted and monitored at all levels.

8.2 Discussion

1) Monitoring

Monitoring, or regulating performance, is an ongoing process. It means that the subject leader will run an ongoing check on the success or otherwise of policies. Monitoring involves checking on what is actually happening. The reasons for monitoring are:

1) to unify the team in continuing to promote effective learning clustered around agreed principles and goals

2) to provide evidence for praise and success

3) to record and celebrate achievement

4) to find out what works well and to use ways of continuing to improve, on the basis of this knowledge.

For the monitoring to be effective it needs to be tied into the vision for the subject which links to the school's overall vision and mission, and the subject leader needs to feel ownership of the issues because he or she has chosen them. In addition to creating the secure environment the subject leader needs to concentrate on small, achievable areas and he or she needs to be totally committed to acting on results. The monitoring needs to be regarded as a real and ongoing part of team practice and not simply as an artificial 'bolt-on' that has been imposed, either internally or externally.

Field *et al* (2000, p138) define monitoring as 'the collection of information about an action or activity'. They compare this with the process of review, which they define as 'the making of decisions about what action, if any, to take as a consequence of the decision reached through evaluation'. They argue that the monitoring, evaluation and review processes, when managed well, can be a very effective learning experience for the team. If the monitoring process is integrated into a genuinely reflective learning environment, it can be a meaningful activity. Both the outcomes and process of monitoring can support staff development. In a truly collegial team culture a subject leader could simply be the facilitator to the monitoring process and allow the team to monitor itself.

In the last chapter we explored the ways in which formulating an effective learning policy can focus a team on learning as the central purpose of all activities, so that staff and pupils can work together to improve the quality of learning for all. We discussed the fact that learning cannot and must not be seen as dislocated from other classroom contexts, outcomes and assessments. In the same way, it is important to think about monitoring, evaluation and review as intrinsically linked to policy formation and implementation. We should see these quality assurance procedures as feeding directly into learning and teaching and not being separate from those activities.

Much of the focus of a monitoring exercise will be based on building up a view of what actually happens in a subject team regarding teaching and learning. In chapter 5 we examined some of the inherent complexities facing a subject leader who may be in a senior position to more experienced teachers. This is nowhere more of a challenge than in the process of monitoring. You need to be aware that some members of your team may feel threatened by monitoring activities and classroom observations in particular. The issue of power and responsibility is highlighted in the literature on quality assurance and time should be spent in creating the secure professional atmosphere that will enable the monitoring to take place without allowing these feelings of insecurity to grow.

You might consider pairing up with another subject leader from a different curriculum subject in order to share reflections and give mutual support. The idea of support for the subject leader as well as for the team is an important one. The resulting professional conversations should also allow subject leaders to put the necessary distance between themselves and their teams.

Teamwork is very important in this context as is a conceptual understanding of how the policy will impact on practice. As West (1998, p35) puts it, 'The policy represents the "public map" of intentions concerning practice. The policy will surface in classrooms where it reflects the "private image" of that policy as perceived by individual teachers.'

Therefore it is really important that it is not just regarded as a blueprint for practice. The idea of extended professionalism, by definition, results in different positions on pedagogical issues and different interpretations of policy. Account must be taken of this in the monitoring and evaluation process. Bell and Ritchie (1999, p39) point out that 'As well as being a formative process... auditing and monitoring should be overt and supportive'. This links to the ideas raised above on thinking about the organic nature of learning and assessment, policy implementation and practice. You should keep in mind your team's understanding of formative assessment when setting up monitoring and evaluation strategies. Monitoring, evaluation and review must not be seen as summative processes: when carried out properly they have all the benefits of formative assessment.

This conceptual understanding must also apply to the quality assurance process. As Harris *et al* (2002, p38) says, 'Both monitoring and evaluation are discrete though inter-related activities which need to be understood fully before attempting to undertake them within the department'.

As we have seen, the processes should be seen not just as formative but as having a direct impact on day-to-day practice. Field *et al* (2002, p186) warn against concentrating just on outcomes as a purpose for the monitoring activities: 'Such a narrow view of evaluation methods can, indeed, have a detrimental effect in that individual teachers can neglect the benefits of process-based issues in favour of examination results'. And it is this deep-level thinking that makes monitoring a useful activity.

If the monitoring is ongoing, routine feedback on how aims are being met can be used to help the team to continually review its work. It is a good idea not to see monitoring as a hierarchical arrangement – as something subject leaders 'do to' the teachers in their team. Rather it should be seen in terms of partnership between colleagues – a team effort. As West puts it (1998, p63) 'an expression of partnership between co-professionals'.

Part of your challenge is to encourage members of your team to recognise the monitoring work that they are already doing as part of their work and general professional practice. Monitoring is, in fact, a natural progression from good reflective practice. The problem is that it is not always possible to carve out the time for this reflection to take place.

In the course of the monitoring process we, as a team and as individuals, come to an understanding of particular and general aspects of practice. Field *et al* (2001, p202) takes up this view: 'Subject leaders, though, are able to work against such short-termism. By motivating teachers to engage actively in the learning process through enquiry and research, they are promoting an ethos of learning... Quality assurance involves teacher quality, learner quality and a general ethos and ambiance of motivation and stimulation.'

West (1998, p35) concurs: 'Teaching and learning is a complex process and it would be foolish to think that just because we have a written policy it is a simple matter for staff to adopt what it contains.'

It is somewhat disingenuous, therefore, to make these points about the organic relationship between monitoring and practice and to present these arguments in a chapter dedicated to quality assurance which is separate from the rest of the book. The reality is, though, that most subject leaders will initially think about the processes separately before integrating them in practice. We need to think about learning as central to the quality assurance process as much as we would with all the other areas of policy implementation.

2) Evaluation

Evaluation encompasses reflecting on the status of the departmental plan's objectives. For subject leaders the evaluation of the departmental plans and policies can provide the basis for action and strategic intervention. Where evaluation works best it can provide the catalyst for changes which will have a positive effect upon the department and departmental working.

With these potential benefits in mind, West (1998, p45) urges caution against evaluation for the sake of it. 'Evaluation is a labour-intensive activity and should not be engaged in for its own sake. The purpose of engaging in evaluation is not to prove but to improve. The sensitive collection of information should help subject leaders to identify effective practice and areas for improvement. Monitoring is a sensitive issue.'

Blandford (1997, p150) adds: 'In contrast to monitoring, evaluation encompasses reviewing the status of a plan's objectives. Through the evaluation process, managers will determine the need to change objectives, priorities and/or practice.'

For monitoring to be successful, then, it is important that the team has faith in you and that there is a general atmosphere of trust and professional integrity. As we can see from the *Standards*, there is a good deal of macro-political emphasis on monitoring and with the advent of the self-evaluating school this will continue to grow.

This is combined with the introduction of performance management and the increased emphasis on managerial understanding of the teaching and learning processes going on in the school. There has been a significant change in recent times from the old model of management, in which the 'closed door' culture of the school was common, to a more open, publicly accountable atmosphere where peer and hierarchical lesson observations are common.

Key to the evaluation process is the timespan when it takes place. It is important that data is gathered over a period of time – it is not a snapshot of practice. It should inform planning and, although it contributes to accountability issues within the school and with external agencies, this is not its main purpose.

Harris, Allsop and Sparks (2002, p42) say that 'Evaluation provides a basis upon which the subject or department leader is able to make judgments and informed decisions... in essence, evaluation is the process of systematically collecting and analysing information in order to make informed judgments based upon sound evidence'.

The processes involved with teaching and learning are complex and they do not lend themselves easily to measuring mechanisms. It is well documented, then, that what happens is that what is easily measured is subjected to measurement and the rest is ignored. It is a challenge for subject leaders to make sure that they develop evaluation mechanisms that can truly reflect the quality of the work that goes on in school and, where necessary, improve it.

3) Review

Review is the most long-term of the three processes and it involves taking a wide overview of data gathered via the evaluation process and taking stock of the long-term vision for the team and the subject. If monitoring provides the information for evaluation, review uses the outcomes from both of these processes to improve practice directly. The review looks to the future and identifies what needs to be changed and what is going well and can be kept the same. Although the three processes of monitoring, evaluation and review are separate, they are often, and indeed should be, linked. A simplistic model of one process happening after the other one has finished, however, is not realistic. More likely, the three processes happen at the same time in different areas and they overlap in a way that is somewhat messy but which is useful for the subject leader's deepening understanding of the challenges facing his or her subject as well as helping him or her to gain a better picture of what is going really well and what needs to be celebrated.

In this way the three processes are not only interdependent but also mutually beneficial. Not only does monitoring provide information for the evaluation but also, as the review is constructed, the team can refine their ideas about what to monitor and which of the data already gathered from the evaluation it is the priority to examine. This means that there can be a two-way traffic between all the processes involved in monitoring, evaluation and review – a dialogue about the findings as the processes go along. This not only informs the process and the learning of the individuals taking part but it also increases the motivation for completing the review.

8.3   Operational

We have explored why monitoring, review and evaluation should not be seen as discrete 'bolt-on' practices. It is important that the method for monitoring and collecting data is agreed at the point of setting up the process. The monitoring processes are not just vehicles for reflecting on practice but learning activities in themselves. One of the major problems with quality assurance activities is the sheer amount of time they take up. If clear schemes of work and a policy for effective learning are already in place, though, monitoring can take place in the time that hitherto was taken up by those activities. LSAs can also do observations and collect pupil viewpoints.

Harris, Allsop and Sparks (2002, p73) state that 'By reviewing monitoring systems the department will be assured that they will receive accurate feedback about the way in which resources are used in the department. Similarly, routine monitoring systems will provide feedback on the extent to which departmental objectives are being met in practice. Evaluation is also a major contributor to departmental and subject planning.'

This can happen more easily when the benefits of monitoring are clearly understood by the team and there is agreement about the reasons for doing it. One, often understated, benefit is that subject leaders can, through monitoring and evaluation and review, be informed about the staff development needs of the time.

Monitoring may also assist middle managers in planning to meet staff learning needs by providing an insight into the strengths and weaknesses in their departments/teams. Other benefits are not so much a matter of choice and more a matter of necessity. We need to monitor, evaluate and review policies in order to see if they were successful.

8.4　The practicalities of monitoring

1) Data collection

As subject leaders we need to consider the type and nature of data to be collected. Ask yourself the following questions about data before it is collected:

- Is it going to further my understanding of the quality of learning in this area?
- Does it tell me something that I can't find anywhere else?
- Do I have a clear idea of what I will do with it once I have it?

When you have clear answers to these questions you can begin to think about how you will go about gathering the data. There are a variety of methods for monitoring. They include:

- classroom observation
- discussions with students
- examination of students' work
- analysis of exam and test results and other value added data on pupils' academic performance
- discussions with staff
- talking to pupils about their perceptions of the subject
- scrutiny of work
- review of teachers' planners.

Self-evaluating departments value the process of self-evaluation and have an accurate and in-depth understanding of where their own strengths and weaknesses lie.

It should be stressed, though, that when a list of characteristics such as this is presented, the impression can be given that in fact complex processes such as monitoring and evaluation are relatively simple. Of course, this is not the case. We will now examine the one that subject leaders often worry about: classroom observation.

Lesson observations

First agree on the basic rules with the team.

1) Where will the subject leader sit, what and how will they write down; will they be introduced to the group?
2) Should the subject leader be 'invisible' or get involved with the students?

It is essential that teachers operate in a secure learning environment as well as the students, and transparency is key to achieving this. It is also important to establish how the information will be used once it has been collected and who will have access to it. Earlier in this book we saw how important it is to establish the nature of the audience when writing policies. This is just as important for any written information collected as part of a monitoring process. You should also take a sophisticated approach to sharing information internally. It is not the case that an internal audience is always less threatening than an external audience so subject leaders should take full account of the subtle dynamics in a team when deciding whether or not to share information.

In the lesson make notes on the following:
- The security of the learning environment.
- How assessment data is used in the lesson.
- How the learning progresses.

'Points for discussion' is a good starting point rather than negative comments because it allows you to ask questions rather than simply making criticisms.

It does not matter how useful and detailed your observation notes are if you do not give effective feedback to the teacher who has been observed.

The four principles of effective feedback

1) Effective learning is highly reliant on an appropriate emotional state on the part of the learner (in this case, the classroom teacher). The emotional state which fosters effective learning is a product of a secure, positive relationship between learner and observer.

2) Assessment and learning processes are inextricably linked and each affects the other in an organic, developmental way. Feedback must be sensitive to the needs of the learner.

3) The dialogue between subject leadership and the learner is fundamental to the process of effective feedback. The quality of feedback is crucial to the quality of the learning and the reflective conversation is at the heart of the learning process.

4) The verbal feedback process, when managed well, can help the learner to verbalise and to consolidate their own learning which may well go beyond the knowledge of the subject leader. This is a cause for celebration and should not be regarded as a threat.

Task 28	Points for inclusion in a lesson observation proforma

TEAM TASK

Use the four principles of effective feedback to construct a lesson observation proforma to be used for monitoring activities. Use any of the following headings, in any order, as well as some of your own to construct the proforma:
- Quality of student learning
- Quality of learning environment
- Evidence of progression
- Evidence of promotion of meta-learning?
- Assessment linked to learning objectives?

Learning is as much the goal of monitoring as it is of assessment and classroom observation. As West (1998, p58) says, 'Policy-related observation is essentially a developmental process... Monitoring assumes a relationship between feedback and development and is predicated on the assumption that staff are willing to take responsibility for their own learning. Constructive focusing on a specific aspect should foster the kind of persistent dialogue that can act as a spur to individual experiment.'

As we saw in the previous chapter, the culture of ongoing professional dialogue in which policy and research are given as much attention as practice should be the long-term goal of the subject leader interested in creating the 'learning subject team'. The dialogue about feedback and observation can be the perfect platform for this.

West (1998, p58) says, 'If the outcomes of the various observations are not brought into productive relationship it will not be possible to refer to policy implementation or the implementation of schemes of work in a rigorous way and the opportunity for institutional learning will be diminished... It is useful to construe institutional learning as team learning. The essence of team learning is dialogue.' He also argues (1998, p33) that we should be comfortable with the concept of repertoire: 'Repertoire has proved to be a useful term of reference in the context of monitoring, since it enables us to proceed from a position in which no one has a "perfect repertoire" and the idea of a preferred teaching style has been dispersed with.'

2) Developing an action plan for data collection

Once these firm protocols have been agreed upon, an action plan can be developed for collecting the data.

The following activities can be used:
■ classroom observation
■ scrutiny of plans
■ conversations with teachers
■ conversations with students
■ video/audio clips of students in lessons
■ examination of pupils' work
■ post-lesson discussion and feedback (to encourage reflective practice).

3) Quantitative data

It sounds like a simple thing to say, but attainment scores are only useful if they actually mean something. If not they tell no bigger story than the one that says what a student achieved in a particular task on a particular day. Also there is the whole range of quantitative data that can be generated by summative assessment. Field *et al* (2001, p194) argues that 'The monitoring of learning is not an exact science, yet the lack of precision should not lead to inactivity. There is no doubt that interest in progress is motivating and stimulating to both teachers and pupils.'

While observing the lesson, subject leaders could change their focus on a range of pedagogical aims. Ideally teams should take joint responsibility for development of observation criteria. Also remember to look at and take account of the learning environment in physical and psychological terms.

4) Putting it all together

In order to make the best use of data gathered from monitoring activities, subject leaders should think about these points:

- What do pupils bring to the school in terms of previous knowledge, ie, 'baseline' information?
- What do pupils gain from the classroom experience that adds to this baseline data?
- It is vital to compare pupils' achievements in different ways using school, local and national data. In other words, to obtain a classroom and a school exceeding perspective.
- It is important not to lose sight of the main reason for engaging in the monitoring and evaluation activities: to find out what works well and what needs to be improved.

Field *et al* (2001, p187) says, 'Planning, monitoring and evaluation must therefore take account of the variables and a range of data-gathering techniques should be employed.' Subject leaders should continue to ask what they are finding out and what issues emerge from the data. They should continue to think about what they are finding out before they get to the final stage of the evaluation process – which is to write the report.

Task 29	Creating a monitoring schedule

TEAM TASK

Use the ideas in this chapter to work together to create a monitoring schedule and a lesson observation proforma. These should grow out of a policy on monitoring, evaluation and review; it is most important that the team agree on quality assurance procedures rather than feeling threatened by them.

8.5 Summary

- Arrangements for monitoring, evaluation and review should be made as part of the strategic planning process.
- Subject leaders need to work hard to ensure that the environment is sufficiently secure for members of the team not to feel threatened by the monitoring process.
- The monitoring process can be made more meaningful if it is regarded as part of the professional learning process.
- If a reflective practitioner approach is taken, all members of the team can learn and grow from the processes involved in monitoring, evaluation and review.
- All policies will be monitored, evaluated and reviewed and either this should be stated in the policies themselves or a separate quality assurance policy needs to be created.

Combining external and internal policy: building capacity for change

Chapter 9

Objectives

By the end of the chapter you will have:

- considered some suggestions as to how subject leaders can build the capacity for change in their teams

- explored the ways that change can be anticipated and managed

- looked at the change process and its effect on a team in more detail

- considered the ways that policies can support staff in their responses to the change process

- explored how teachers can be empowered within such circumstances

- examined the internal factors of effective teams able to adapt to change and maintain professional integrity.

9.1 Discussion

'Change is not made without inconvenience, even from worse to better.' So wrote Samuel Johnson in 1755. The sentiment is as true today as it was then. The management of any change process demands high-level professional and personal skills. As a subject leader implementing policies, you will always be involved in the change process because you will be responding to internal and external pressures. Although the *Standards for Subject Leaders* (TTA, 1998) do not have a great deal to say about the specific skills involved in managing change in a subject team, the general assumption that all other leadership tactics will take place in a changing environment pervades the text. Change is presented as an inescapable reality, for example on p6: 'The knowledge and understanding required will change over time and it is important that subject leaders recognise their responsibility to remain up to date with developments in the subject area and in other aspects of education reality to their role.' So change is a given; it is a continuous reality. In the third paragraph of the introduction to the *Standards* the philosophical basis for standards is set out: 'Although the subject leader must have a good knowledge of the subject, these standards focus primarily on expertise in the leadership and management of the subject' (p3). The management of change is generally agreed to be a feature of management and leadership knowledge.

The fact is that these are rapidly changing times. This is because of deliberate political intervention as well as incremental societal changes such as the increase in single households and the use of computers in the home and workplace. The life expectancy of people in developed countries has changed and is continuing to change rapidly. Our traditional view of education – that most of it happens before the age of 16 – needs to change accordingly. Changes are numerous: they are social, economic, political, cultural and biological. The advent of e-learning is just one of the massive changes that will have a continuing effect on the teaching profession in the near future. Because the majority of teachers work in the state sector they are publicly funded and because of this they will always be on the receiving end of interventions generated by national governments and local authorities. This fact must be the starting-point of any discussions about how subject leaders can manage change. But it must certainly not be the end of the story. Professionalism is a difficult term to define. Most people would agree, however, that a major factor in professionalism is the right and ability of a profession to define its own knowledge base and to have a significant degree of autonomy over its working life.

This chapter will attempt to offer you some guidelines concerning how you can manage this balance while retaining your own professional integrity and the integrity of the subject. It is not meant to be an excuse for the rapid – sometimes seemingly relentless – changes instigated by governments. It is, rather, a way of negotiating a path through these changes and even finding advantages within them. Leadership and change are axiomatic. The leadership of change is not a discrete skill but intrinsic to the leader's role. We are often presented with the notion that senior and middle leaders need to learn how to lead and manage change. In the 1980s, for example, change was often presented as an event: something that happened once and was accommodated. This, though, was a misrepresentation. Change is, in fact, a systematic process. We need to accept this as a starting point. None of us can manage change; all we can manage is our own responses to change, while protecting others in our team from the ravages of change as well as taking some control of the changes we invoke.

As we have seen, all change involves a degree of stress and this can be negative or positive. On the other hand, learning is always about change. So the impact of change on a team or an institution will always be both profound and complex. Some psychologists say that we always go back to the major milestones in our life whenever we encounter smaller change situations in our work or personal lives. As a subject leader, your attempts to change will clearly be not just about the implementation of change but also people's difficult psychological reactions to it.

Given the way that change can lead to fatigue and negativity, it is startling how much change has gone on in education in the last two decades. And yet it could be argued that, given the sheer amount of energy that has been expended on implementing these changes, it is staggering that so little has actually changed. Despite millions of pounds of public money being spent, hours of teachers' work, numerous versions of public documents, not much has actually changed. Essentially, children still go to school between the ages of five and 16 or 18, between about 8.30am and 3.30pm, five days a week, at an institution where they are taught in classrooms with approximately 30 of their peers, by adults. Given the massive advances in neurobiology, understanding of child development, technology and changes in working and life patterns of the past 20 years, we could argue that the scandal of government intervention into education is not that there has been too much but that there has been too little.

A lot has been written in leadership literature about the 'management of change' but, as we have established, change can never really be managed. Change is part of the nebulous and sometimes chaotic reality that was mentioned in the first chapter. All that can be managed is one's own response to the change and, to a certain extent, the responses of one's team.

The brain works with precedents – repeating established ways of seeing the world and patterns of behaviour that emanate from it – rather than with novelty or new events. The knowledge that dealing with your team's mixed responses to change is bound up with their personal histories may help you to not take the hostility so personally but it does not present you with an easy situation. We all carry around our personal histories on our backs like invisible tortoise shells. When faced with a new situation our mind finds a similar situation in the records it has of our past and often causes us to act in a pattern of behaviour that was established in response to an apparently disconnected event.

So although the act of implementing a new government strategy or changing school sites may not appear to have much in common with how we felt as five-year-olds starting school, the mind may resort to those feelings of abandonment and defensiveness because that is how we have dealt with every other new situation in our life. The brain is designed for survival and it responds to a threat in the same way whether the threat is a baying wild animal or a government policy on a new assessment system. This is why change often produces feelings of loss of control.

So the more the subject leader can create a safe environment, the better – and effective, shared, well thought-out policies can help you to do this. Sometimes the need for control is best served by recognising that striving for it is futile. This may sound harsh but you should give up trying to control the change and instead stick to supporting the team in their dealings with the change process.

The constructivist view of learning is that we as human beings are always in the process of making meaning. It is this constant activity that gives us our sense of self and our place in the world. In order to make meaning effectively we need to have a frame of reference in which to decode the multiple and varied messages that we receive on a daily basis. It is your frame of reference that informs your sense of self and helps you to define who you are. If your frame of reference is that you are naturally a 'people' person, that you value kind and supportive friendships with others and that you take your popularity for granted, the inherent unpopularity that accompanies some aspects of management may be very hard for you to bear in the first few months of being a subject leader.

Alternatively, if you have always achieved highly in an individualistic way and have successfully competed with other people, your new role as subject leader and the necessary onus on team-building and creating a blame-free atmosphere may test your frame of reference and make you re-examine how you define success. In both cases in order to thrive, the wise subject leader needs to change and re-examine some of the beliefs and structures that informed the previous view of the self. When we are under threat we often choose the path of holding on to our frame of reference rather than simply admitting we were wrong.

This is important, not just for you but for the teachers in your team. Forgive the somewhat stereotypical example that follows, but it is worth overstating the case in order to demonstrate the clash of values that results when no policies have been created or no shared vision exists. The example concerns the teacher who sees herself as a benevolent maternal figure whose role is to help the children she regards as less able to feel comfortable about themselves by not challenging them intellectually. She is faced by a huge dilemma when the subject leader has to question her about the starkly low attainment scores of her classes – especially, as the value added data reveals, of those children from low social and economic backgrounds. The subject leader may have the opinion that the teacher's compliance with underachievement is depriving already impoverished children of a chance of an equal stake in society and the government's inclusion agenda endorses this.

In this situation the subject leader needs to get the teacher to change but he or she is up against more than just a change of practice in an experienced professional. For in order for this teacher to change her practice enough to meet national expectations, the teacher needs to address her own value system and sense of self. The wise subject leader needs to realise this. If she is strong enough the experienced teacher may be able to reassess her original assumptions and either come to the conclusion that they were wrong or she may find a way of reinterpreting her kind, philanthropic feelings about her charges and still work within the new philosophy. If she is not strong enough to do this she will continue to think her interpretation of the world is the only one and that everybody else is wrong. Unfortunately this may involve some disciplinary interventions for which the subject leader will need the support of senior management.

Whatever the situation, then, the subject leader needs to understand that these feelings will always be a feature of the individual and the team reactions to change and the wise subject leader makes time and space for these feelings to be articulated before moving on to the practicalities of implementing the change. People need to feel secure enough to articulate their feelings of self-doubt and apparent incompetence in the face of change. But this does not mean that the subject leader always needs to toe the party line. With outside changes it is possible to take a 'let's try it' attitude without compromising one's principles if the vision has genuinely informed the team's policies. Part of the reason for creating the secure learning environment lies in the research into learning organisations.

There has been a good deal of work in the business sector about organisational learning and although normally we should exercise caution when importing such ideas into education, it is worth thinking about how other professions build the capacity for change. Denton (1998, p91) identifies nine characteristics of organisational learning:

1) learning strategy
2) flexible structure
3) blame-free culture
4) vision
5) external awareness
6) knowledge creation and transfer
7) quality
8) supportive atmosphere
9) team working.

Learning is fundamental to building the capacity for change in an organisation. It should be habitual and a fundamental part of every person's job. Vision is also vital for capacity for change, and for challenging the assumptions that go to make up the status quo. Sometimes it is not so much change that is the threat as the status quo: we often deny the pernicious effects of present circumstances in order to resist transformation, even though the alternative maybe better for us. As we established in chapter 4, shared vision can help to change the status quo. In negotiating the path between change and the status quo, the team becomes highly important. The collective skills of the team can be pooled to articulate existing knowledge but also to create new knowledge. The learning organisation is not in denial or resistance about the fact that change is ongoing and inevitable.

We need to recognise that the environment is in a state of continual change. The more change that a team is faced with, the more important external awareness becomes. A key form of learning is to anticipate change and thus be ready to adapt if and when change takes place. Williams (1995) makes the point that because of the dramatic changes to the education system since the mid-1980s teamwork is now a permanent part of teachers' way of working. Combined knowledge is as important to the learning strategy of the team and organisation as its general capacity to change.

Teamwork creates its own culture but it also reflects the overall culture of the school. School culture is a vital component in how individual teachers react to change. School improvement literature stresses the importance of school culture in the rate and effectiveness of improvement. In terms of school improvement, the capacity to improve is actually more important than current academic outcomes. Part of dealing with change is about dealing with conflict. In some schools, the friendly, supportive culture can actually be counterproductive to change because teachers do not want to risk spoiling the status quo by voicing contradictory points of view. Subject leaders need to encourage frank discussion where things are not taken personally if there is a disagreement. In fact, disagreements are encouraged and laughed about. MacGilchrist *et al* (1997, p104) have identified nine intelligences of successful schools which have the ability to change.

Nine intelligences of successful schools

1) contextual intelligence

2) strategic intelligence

3) academic intelligence

4) reflective intelligence

5) pedagogical intelligence

6) collegial intelligence

7) emotional intelligence

8) spiritual intelligence

9) ethical intelligence

| Task 30 | Using the nine intelligences |

TEAM TASK

Use the list above as a starting-point for a policy on how the team deals with change. You might want to start by turning each intelligence into a question with which to interrogate each change agent. For example, a question linked to point 1 (contextual intelligence) might be 'Have you thought about how this change will be implemented in this school where 75% of pupils receive free school meals?'

The more of these intelligences that are in place, the higher the capacity of the school to cope with and initiate change effectively. These can also be applied to the subject leader and subject team.

Blandford (1997, p176) identifies three types of change: top-down, bottom-up and expert. The subject leader is subject to all three types.

Where the culture is ready for change there are often common characteristics present. You should try to bear these in mind:

1) A previous history of successful innovations will help team members to put their faith in the change.

2) Consultation which is genuine will help team members own the change and implement it with more investment.

3) A respected change agent (subject leader) will have more chance of effecting the change with the backing of the team than one who is not respected.

4) All change must be accompanied with an appropriate time for maintenance and bedding down.

5) Communication is the key to success throughout the process.

In terms of the practicalities of managing change, clarity is paramount.

9.2 Operational

| Task 31 | How do you deal with change? |

INDIVIDUAL TASK

First establish what your own pattern of responses to change is. This will help you to locate your own feelings and so prepare the ground for you to take your colleagues through the change process. In each of the following boxes, give an example of how you have felt about change in the past and how you have behaved in the face of change. You can add your own examples to the ones below.

Life change	Feelings associated	Behaviour
Going to university	eg Superficially happy but very worried	eg Overused alcohol, settled down after a while etc
Change of job		
Becoming a parent		
Moving house		
Others		

You don't need to share this table with anyone else. The point of the exercise is to identify patterns in your behaviour. Have you greeted change with open arms and moved through transitions effortlessly or has each transition in your life been met with conflict or depressed feelings? Nobody is pretending that a new software system is comparable to the big life changes above, but your responses to these milestones will give you some indication of how you will deal with the small issues that face you professionally.

Now we can turn to how you can manage the responses to change in your team.

Your first priority is to establish what it is that you and your team most value about your work. In other words, what is your shared philosophy of teaching the subject? Previous chapters should have led you to a greater understanding of this. Go back to your responses to the earlier individual tasks in the book to remind yourself how to approach change and use the draft of the policy for dealing with change above as a guideline (see task 30). A key aspect of the team's learning is how to anticipate and recognise change.

Task 32	Anticipating the big changes

TEAM TASK

The purpose of this task is to encourage the team to think deeply about possible developments that may have an impact on teaching and learning in the future.

Delegate researching different aspects of the anticipated changes to the subject team. The changes should be divided into levels:

Level 1 = internal – changes likely to be dictated by the school development plan, the post-Ofsted action plan and mission statement

Level 2 = external – government strategies, the Race Relations Amendment Act, other acts

Level 3 = technological – computer software available in the classroom, in homes and as professional tools

Level 4 = environmental – includes changes to the site and to local demographics, and wider changes in population and profession.

Use the pie chart below to plot team's ideas about policy changes that will have an impact on team practice in the next 10 years. This is not to say that the team can expect to be in their posts for the next 10 years, but knowledge of possible changes should have some impact on practice.

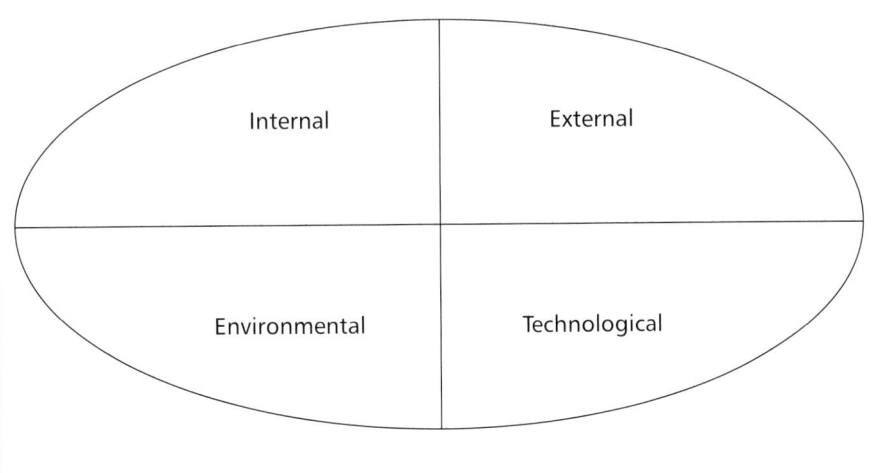

Ask members of the team to bring what they find out about these levels to a team meeting. Discuss where the subject fits into all this – you will be surprised to find out what it reveals. Use the rest of the information in this chapter to divide the changes into threats and opportunities and those which will be brought in from a top-down or bottom-up perspective.

9.3 Summary

- Change is messy and continuous. It is neither logical nor linear.
- We all bring a lot of baggage to the way we react to change.
- You cannot manage change but you can lead other people in their responses to it and set an example by understanding your own response to change.
- The stronger and more vibrant the team ethos, the better the individuals in the team can deal with change.
- If the policies are genuinely shared and if they genuinely articulate the vision for the subject, change can be measured against fixed principles and thus be made more meaningful.

Where next?

10.1 Introduction

This final chapter is about the way forward. It is an opportunity to pause for a moment to consider where all this work on subject leadership and policy-writing leaves us. We ask whether subject leadership as a concept is one that will endure – and when all the political and contextual pressures are stripped away, we'll ask what matters most to you, as a subject leader. It is also a good point for you to ask, where next? Transformation means setting new parameters. Schools can only improve so much and only be so effective within a framework. Maybe the time has come to devise a new framework – one which is determined by subject leaders and teachers themselves. That really would be professional.

The 1990s saw a sharp increase in interest in the twin concepts of school effectiveness and school improvement. The promises that these movements made about how profound institutional changes could be brought about by powerful and effective school leadership were beguiling to politicians who, after a decade were still at a loss as to how to deliver results to a public that was represented in the press as dissatisfied about state education. Partly, this interest was also a reaction against the crude and often cruel performance tables of the early 90s which proved no more, in many cases, than could be predicted by matching areas of low social and economic indicators and poor school performance.

The very idea of a direct link between 'good leadership' and 'outcomes' is, itself, very strongly linked to the New Labour vision. Blair's leadership, it has been said (Hutton, 1999) is more controlling and shaping than that of any other British prime minister in recent history. The identity of its leader infiltrates the New Labour government at all levels and is certainly evident in the *Standards for Subject Leaders* (TTA, 1998). Previous ways of regarding leadership might have examined it in terms of the leader's ability to foster good relations within the team or by encouraging others to produce 'good work', but not linked the quality of leadership so strongly to 'outcomes'. In this way, although the foundations were laid down for them previously, the *Standards for Subject Leaders* are intrinsically a New Labour text.

School improvement and school effectiveness also held great appeal for the New Labour government because some of the inherent ideas coincided perfectly with the onus on leadership that characterised much of the New Labour style. It is easy to see how the identification of school effectiveness with powerful leadership appealed to New Labour in its first term of government. It has been noted that never before has a party invested so much of its identity in its leader. Tony Blair is not only a major component of the New Labour brand; he is interchangeable with it. But with nice synchronicity, just as it emerged that the much publicised 'superheads' that were the natural conclusion of school improvement research findings were, one by one, shown to be failing, so New Labour, in its second term, has become increasingly beleaguered by charges of 'spin'.

The personality cult that defines superheads and prime ministers has been increasingly shown to be problematic at best and vacuous at worst. In both cases the need for a more collective or 'distributed' approach to leadership has become apparent.

There are three problems with the school improvement and school effectiveness movements having a direct impact on policy. The first is that they oversimplify complex, context-specific ideas into bullet-pointed soundbites by using lists of characteristics of, for example, effective and improving schools. This has meant that the ideas which are argued elegantly and rigorously at length in academic journals have been imported in their simplest terms into the macro-political arena.

When an effort is made for these ideas to have immediate and widescale impact, the second problem arises: complex learning processes are supplanted by easily measurable outcomes. In this way, the apparently 'teacher-friendly' value added agenda has been as hard a taskmaster on schools as the earlier 'raw data' way of scoring achievement. The trend, started in the mid-80s, has not only been challenged but added to – that is, the testing agenda is now paramount. The corollary is that what is measured defines what is taught. This legacy of the school improvement movement's need for raw data against which to add the value of teacher input has, ironically, become a burden on the teachers whose work it seeks to celebrate.

The third and final problem with the school improvement movement is the one that is illustrated in the *Standards for Subject Leaders:* that is, the conflation of middle and subject leadership. The concentration on high-level senior leadership skills in the mid-90s meant that, for a long time, subject and middle leadership were simply ignored. In the past two or three years there has been a more concerted recognition of the vital importance of those in middle management and also an admission that the skills involved in the work of subject leaders are different from those required by senior managers.

We have reached a point now where we have a more sophisticated understanding of how learning is different from outcome and how the measurement of attainment by test results not only gives a limited view of the learning but can even be detrimental to the learning process. Black and Wiliam's (1998) masterly overview of the assessment research is continuing to have an impact on practitioners' understanding of formative assessment and the general underpinning notion that assessment data is worthless if it does not have a direct impact on learning and teaching processes. Even Ofsted, once thought to be the purveyor of grades and outcomes, takes the idea of assessment for learning seriously.

The challenge for you as a subject leader is now to reconcile your knowledge of, and, perhaps, sympathy for the developments in learning and assessment theory, some of which will run counter to the prevailing macro-political climate, while steering a safe course for your subject and your team.

Finding ways of celebrating and measuring the learning processes going on in the classroom is a challenge, certainly, but the rewards are numerous. It starts with a genuine and general commitment to the learning by the team. This can steer the apparently bureaucratic aspects of the job, rather than running counter to them. If you can provide students with the vocabulary with which to talk about their learning, they can begin to take some responsibility for genuine self-assessment. You can also influence your team to be able to recognise active learning as opposed to the vaguer concept of being 'on task' or, worse, mistaking good behaviour for learning. If we can recognise what it looks like we can also build the conditions that will support it.

If we are really going to take learning seriously, we need to embrace the idea that schools are not the only significant learning arena. This means embracing the idea of learning for all, across age boundaries. Lifelong learning has become something of a cliché but this should not detract from the fact that it is not just a good idea but it is crucial to our development as a society. For you, the subject leader, this means thinking about yourself and your team as learners first and teachers second. It means thinking about the students you teach as learners who are engaged in learning how to learn as well as learning about your subject.

Part of this wider understanding of lifelong learning is our fresh perspective on professional development. For a long time teachers had two conflicting influences on their professional development, neither of which were satisfactory.

The first has been the traditional route of advancement through studying for a higher degree in education such as an MA. Many teachers who have completed higher degrees will testify how useful and satisfying an activity this is. You get to meet other teachers and share ideas, as well as engaging in research. The only problem with this sort of study is that it is not directly linked to career development and although lots of teachers who have used their master's degrees to further their careers it has been up to them, the teachers, to make the connection. For many years in education promotion was not discussed and professional learning in this context was dislocated from career development. The second type of professional work offered has been the one-off, government-funded Inset day. This sort of thing can be useful in solving short-term training needs such as the implementation of a new ICT system but it is not a good model of teaching and learning because it is not negotiated, not ongoing and does not provide space for reflection. Inset days are training rather than education opportunities.

The *Standards* have gone a long way to bringing the dual needs of teachers' career development and professional learning together because the advancement is clearly marked in stages. Although the *Standards* are not perfect (as we have seen throughout the book) they represent the first serious attempt by a government to structure teachers' professional development in a serious way and this is a massive step forward.

If you, as a subject leader, take learning seriously as part of your professional role, it is fitting that professionalism is taken equally seriously. Part of this is reclaiming the right to define professional knowledge and use professional vocabulary.

In the last couple of decades professional vocabulary has increasingly been defined for teachers by the government. 'Key skills', 'Sats' and 'baseline' are all terms frequently used by teachers but they are also terms that have been given to the profession by the government. Coupled with the somewhat out-of-date but residual antipathy towards 'theory' in the profession, this has meant that there has been an absence of professional vocabulary. This is changing and it can be changed further by adopting the language of learning to embrace meta-learning in the profession. As a subject leader you are in a good position to set the tone for the subject team.

Throughout the book we have looked at the different ways of regarding definitions of management and leadership. We have examined the limitations of perceiving them as completely separate sets of activities and considered the way that they are inextricably linked and overlapping. The truth is, though, that as far as the subject leader is concerned none of this really matters. The fact is that the activities associated with leading and managing are pretty much intermingled. It is impossible to write a policy effectively without leading your team in its construction.

One thing is for certain, though: however you define its activities, the role of the subject leader is set to increase in its sphere of influence in the next few years. It is not only NQTs and student teachers that you will be working with but also the significant contribution made by other adults – learning support assistants (LSAs) will make a significant contribution to work in schools.

Although there are things to be concerned about in governmental terms, there are also signs that things are changing for the better. Ofsted has said that the best-ever cohort of NQTs is now in the profession, and whatever that means, it does at least signify a change in the way that the government is talking to and about the profession. Jane Davison, the minister for education in Wales, has taken a major step to dismantle some of the more draconian apparatus of state education in that country, such as league tables.

So, in this sense at least, times are good. In fact, they have never been better for subject leaders in terms of career development. You might want to consider a diploma in subject leadership before going on to an NPQH, or you may wish to pursue an MA, EdD or PhD.

10.2 Where next?

So where do you go from here? Hopefully you will continue to engage with government policy and continue to work with your team in the creation and implementation of policies. Throughout this book we have examined the link between learning, teaching and leading. If you want to continue your own learning, here are some more details about formal learning opportunities that you might want to take up:

Post-graduate diploma in subject leadership

This postgraduate diploma which runs over the duration of two years combines academic study of subjects such as leadership and management of change with professional development as structured by the *Standards for Subject Leadership*. It allows you to reflect on your own leadership role while developing a deeper understanding of the research about leadership. The diploma is taught at master's level and you have the opportunity to 'upgrade' the diploma to a master's degree by adding a dissertation.

Master's degree in education

The master's degree is one of the most popular options for teachers wanting to develop their professional learning in an academic context. There are hundreds of topics for study at master's level – from museum and environment education to the role of gender in the classroom. Generally master's degrees include some choice of subject matter. Nearly all master's degrees will involve the production of a dissertation. The master's degree will appeal to you if you know that you enjoy meeting and working with others, and structure as well as freedom of learning.

EdD

This is a taught doctorate in which you research a particular area of education over a number of years but you work in a way similar to master's degrees. The EdD will suit you if you have a research interest that you want to pursue at length and depth but you value the 'community of learners' situation that you may have experienced while studying for a master's degree.

PhD

The traditional route to a higher research degree. You produce an extended thesis (usually of between 70,000 and 90,000 words). You work with a supervisor based in a university. The PhD will suit you if you have a clear idea of what you want to research and if you are highly motivated to work on your own.

National Professional Qualification for Headship (NPQH)

Finally, this is a professional qualification that prepares you for headship. You will learn about different concepts involved in headship and management as well as learning about the practical issues involved in headship. This course is for you if you know that you want to proceed up the management route towards headship but you are not interested in having an academic qualification.

Create your own professional development plan. Use the table below to write down what you enjoy about your job and what you find less satisfying.

Task 33	Professional development plan – part 1

INDIVIDUAL TASK

What I enjoy about my role:	What I find less satisfying about my role:

Next plot your medium- and long-term aims. Then list activities you have already undertaken to work towards your goals and then the professional learning activities that you expect to carry out to help you achieve your goals.

| Task 34 | Professional development plan – part 2 |

	Medium-term aims	Professional learning	Long-term aims	Professional learning
Area of interest 1, eg a better knowledge of assessment				
Area of interest 2, eg management leadership				
Area of interest 3				
Area of interest 4				
Area of interest 5				
Area of interest 6				

TEAM TASK

Ask other members of your team to carry out a similar exercise in private. If you are carrying out appraisals, the results could inform those discussions. If not, use the team's reflections to pool team learning objectives.

Finally, good luck in your endeavours with policy-writing as a subject leader. The subject leader's role is absolutely crucial to the way the school runs. The policy-writing process is vitally important to the subject leadership role and the more you can make that experience meaningful for your team, the better the ultimate practice will be. It is only by continuing to learn that we can effectively teach. Whether this means that we, like Chaucer's scholar, will 'gladly learn and gladly teach' or not, the benefits of understanding the struggles and enjoyments of learning are profound.

Bibliography

Ball, S (1994) *Education Reform: a critical and post-structuralist approach*. Milton Keynes: Open University Press

Bell, D, Ritchie, R (1999) *Towards Effective Subject Leadership in the Primary School*. Buckingham: Open University Press

Black, P, Wiliam, D (1998) *Inside the Black Box: raising standards through classroom assessment*. Cambridge: University of Cambridge School of Education and the Assessment Reform Group

Blandford, S (1997) *Middle Management in Schools: how to harmonize managing and teaching for an effective school*. London: Pearson Education

Bloom, BS (ed) (1964) *Taxonomy of Educational Objectives*. London: Longman

Brown, M, MacNamara, O (2001) Initial and Continuing Professional Development of Teachers. In *Teaching and Learning Primary Numeracy: Policy, Practice and Effectiveness*. Nottingham: BERA

Bush, T (2003) *Middle Level Leaders – Think Piece*. www.ncsl.uk/lftm

Clarke, C (2002) Speech made at Oxford University, 30 October 2002

Commission for Racial Equality, The (May 2002) *The Duty to Promote Race Equality: a guide for schools*. www.cre.gov.uk

Commission for Racial Equality, The (2002) *Framework for a race equality policy for schools*. www.cre.gov.uk

Collarbone, P, Billingham, M (1998) Leadership and Our Schools. *School Improvement Research Matters, 8*

Denton, J (1998) *Organisational Learning and Effectiveness*. London: Routledge

DfEE (1999) *Citizenship: The National Curriculum of England*. London: HMSO

DfEE (1999) *The National Curriculum: Handbook for Secondary Teachers*. Sudbury: DfEE

DfEE (1999) *All Our Futures*. London: The Stationery Office

DfEE (2000) *Guidance on Performance Management*. London: The Stationery Office

DfEE (2000) *Professional Development: support for teaching and learning*. Questionnaire and survey, 9 February 2000

DfEE (2000) *National Curriculum*. London: The Stationery Office

DfEE (2001) *National Continuing Professional Development Strategy*. London: DfEE

Docking, J (1999) *National School Policy: Major Issues in Education Policy for Schools in England and Wales, 1979 onwards*. London: David Fulton

Elmore, R (1979) 'Backward mapping: implementation, research and policy decisions'. *Political Science Quarterly*

Eraut, M (1994) *Developing Professional Knowledge and Competences*. London: Falmer Press

Field *et al* (2000) *Effective Subject Leadership*. London: Routledge

Field, K (2002a). 'Evidence Based Subject Leadership'. *Journal of In-Service Education*, vol 28, no 3, pp459-475

Field, K (2004) *Subject Leadership: the Cross-Curriculum*. London: Optimus Publishing

Field, K, Philpott, C (1999) *Subject Mentoring and School Improvement*.
Canterbury: CELSI

Field, K *et al,* (2001) *Subject Leadership – A Key Reference File*. London: Optimus Publishing

Field, K, Holden, P, Lawlor, H (2000). *Effective Subject Leadership*. London: Routledge

Fleming, P (2000) *The Art of Middle Management in Secondary Schools: A Guide to Effective Subject and Team Leadership*. London: David Fulton

Fleming, P, Amesbury, M (2001) *The Art of Middle Management in Primary Schools: A Guide to Effective Subject, Year and Team Leadership*. London: David Fulton

Fullan, M (1991) *The New Meaning of Educational Change*. London: Cassell

Gardner, H (1983) *Frames of Mind: the theory of multiple intelligences*.
New York: Basic Books

General Teaching Council (March 2003) *The Teachers' Professional Learning Framework*.
London and Birmingham: General Teaching Council for England

Glover, D, Miller, D, Gambling, M, Gough, G, Johnson, M (1998)
Subject Leaders: Work, Organisation and Professional Development. Keele: Keele University

Goddard, D, Leask, M (1992) *The Search for Quality: planning for improvement and managing change*. London: Paul Chapman Publishing

Gold, A, Earley, P, Evans, J (2002) *Leadership for transforming learning: NCSL's ten propositions and emergent leaders*. www.ncsl.org.uk

Goleman, D (1996) *Emotional Intelligence: why it matters more than IQ*. London: Bloomsbury

Gunter, HM (2001) *Leaders and Leadership in Education*. London: Paul Chapman Publishing

Hargreaves, D, Hopkins, D (1993) 'School Effectiveness, School Improvement and Development Planning'. In Preedy, M (ed) *Managing the Effective School*. Buckingham: Open University Press

Harris, A, Jamieson, IM, Russ, J (1995) 'A study of 'effective' departments in secondary schools'. *School Organisation*, 15 (3): pp283-299

Harris, A (2001) *Good teaching, effective departments: findings from a HMI survey of subject teaching in secondary schools*, 2000-1. London: Ofsted

Harris, A (1999) *Effective Subject Leadership in Secondary Schools: A Handbook of Staff Development Activities*. London: David Fulton

Harris, A, Jamieson, I, Russ, J (1997) 'A Study of Effective Departments in Secondary Schools'. In Harris, A, Bennett, N, Preedy, M (eds) *Organisational Effectiveness and Improvement in Education*. Buckingham: Open University Press

Harris, A, Allsop, A, Sparks, N (2002) *Leading the Improving Department: A Handbook of Staff Development Activities*. London: David Fulton

Hoyle, E (1995) 'Changing conceptions of a profession'. In Busher, H, Saran, R (eds) *Managing Teachers as Professionals in Schools*. London: Kogan Page

Hughes, S (2004) *Subject Leadership: Resource Management*. London: Optimus Publishing

Hutton, W (1999) *The Stakeholding Society: writings on politics and economics*. Oxford: Polity Press

Johnson, H (1999) 'Performance Management and Targets'. In Docking, J (ed) *National School Policy: Major Issues in Education Policy for Schools in England and Wales, 1979 onwards*. London: David Fulton

Johnson, H (1999) 'School Management and Funding'. In Docking, J (ed) *National School Policy: Major Issues in Education Policy for Schools in England and Wales, 1979 onwards*. London: David Fulton

Lortie, D (1975) *School Teacher: A Sociological Study*. Chicago: University of Chicago Press

MacGilchrist, B, Mortimore, P, Savage, J, Beresford, C (1995) *Planning Matters: The impact of development planning in primary schools*. London: Paul Chapman Publishing

MacGilchrist, B, Myers, K, Reed, J (1997) *The Intelligent School*.
London: Paul Chapman Publishing

Martin, D (1995) 'The National Curriculum and Assessment: a tale of unequal choice and incoherent diversity'. In Williams, V (ed) *Towards Self-Managing Schools*. London: Cassell

Moore, A, Edwards, G, Halpin, D, George, R (2002) 'Resistance and Pragmatism: the (re)construction of schoolteacher identities in a period of intensive educational reform'. *British Educational Research Journal: Journal of the British Educational Research Association*, vol 28, no 4, pp551-567

Office for Standards in Education (1995) *Framework for the Inspection of Schools*. London: HMSO

Ofsted, (2002) *Good Teaching, Effective Departments: Findings for a HMI Survey of Subject Teaching in Secondary Schools, 2000/1*. London: Office for Standards in Education

Rawlings, E (2001) *Changing the Subject: the impact of national policy on school geography 1980-2000*. Sheffield: The Geographical Association

Sammons, P, Hillman, J, Mortimore, P (1995) *Key Characteristics of Effective Schools: a review of school effectiveness research*. Report commissioned by the Office for Standards in Education. London: Institute of Education and Office for Standards in Education

Schön, DA (1983) *The Reflective Practitioner: how professionals think in action*.
London: Basic Books

Sorensen, P, Hoult, E, Philpott, C, Katene, W (2002) 'Peer Learning in Initial Teacher Education (ITE): the use of subject pairing in school experience placements as a strategy for professional learning'. Paper presented at the British Educational Research Association Annual Conference, Exeter University, 12-14 September 2002

Teacher Training Agency (1998) *The Standards for Subject Leaders*. London: TTA

West Burnham, J (2003) *Leadership Beyond School Improvement*. Paper presented at CANTARNET conference, Canterbury Christ Church University College

West, N (1998) *Middle Management in the Primary School: a development guide for curriculum leaders, subject managers and senior staff* (2nd edn). London: David Fulton

Williams, V (1995) *Towards Self-Managing Schools*. London: Cassell

Index

macro policy, 3, 7, 8, 21

masters degrees, 72

meetings, xvi, 11, 23, 62, 69, 70, 71, 72, 73, 76

middle management, xiv, xv, xvi, 1, 3, 4, 17, 25, 43, 44, 45, 46, 47, 49, 50, 54, 58, 94, 99, 100, 102

national curriculum, 6, 7, 13, 15, 16, 19, 22, 24, 26, 28, 31, 44, 61, 62, 99, 100, 102

New Labour, xv, 17, 20, 24, 25, 26, 53, 93

NPQH (National Professional Qualification for Headship), xi, 96, 97

NQT (Newly Qualified Teacher), xi, xv, 20, 49, 53, 68, 69, 96

Ofsted, xi, xiii, 1, 6, 9, 10, 14, 18, 31, 35, 38, 39, 44, 51, 52, 55, 59, 76, 91, 94, 96, 101, 102

open enrolment, 13, 14, 15, 16

pastoral, 3, 4, 5, 17

pedagogy, xiv, 31, 67, 68

performance management, 18, 20, 46, 53, 79, 100, 101

PhD, 96, 97

policies, ix, xv, 2, 3, 6, 7, 8, 10, 11, 14, 16, 19, 20, 21, 23, 24, 25, 26, 27, 28, 29, 30, 33, 35, 36, 37, 39, 40, 41, 43, 47, 50, 51, 53, 55, 56, 57, 58, 59, 60, 63, 65, 66, 71, 72, 73, 75, 76, 77, 79, 81, 82, 84, 85, 87, 88, 92, 96

policy documents, 11, 19, 20, 25, 35, 57, 58, 59

post-16, 15, 30

Post Graduate Diploma in Subject Leadership, 96

professional development, xv, xvi, xvii, 1, 2, 3, 10, 13, 15, 18, 20, 26, 39, 50, 51, 53, 57, 70, 71, 73, 95, 96, 97, 98, 99, 100

professionalism, 13, 18, 20, 24, 26, 57, 59, 70, 78, 86, 95

professional knowledge, 1, 9, 29, 95, 100

professional learning, 2, 18, 57, 69, 70, 84, 95, 96, 98, 100, 102

professional vocabulary, 62, 95

quality, xv, 3, 25, 32, 36, 38, 59, 60, 63, 65, 73, 75, 76, 77, 78, 79, 80, 81, 82, 84, 88, 93, 100

race relations, 13, 14, 19, 91

reflection, 28, 57, 73, 76, 78, 95

research, xv, xvi, 6, 10, 39, 43, 52, 55, 57, 63, 65, 66, 69, 70, 71, 73, 79, 83, 88, 93, 94, 95, 96, 97, 99, 100, 102

resistance, ix, 21, 37, 89, 102

school culture, 10, 19, 35, 36, 51, 53, 89

school effectiveness, 9, 25, 43, 57, 93, 94, 101, 102

school improvement, 4, 9, 10, 17, 22, 25, 27, 39, 43, 44, 66, 70, 89, 93, 94, 99, 100, 101, 102

Sencos, xv, 4, 51

senior management, xiv, 3, 4, 9, 10, 35, 38, 39, 40, 43, 45, 49, 50, 57, 59, 60, 62, 88